T0112662

MAN OF STEEL:

Joseph Stalin

"The objective, thoroughly documented biography of the shoemaker's son who rose from a feudal type of society to become a tyrant with vast powers provides a substantial and highly readable history of development within Russia in this century and of her political relationships with other countries. . . . Clearly interpreted are Stalin's role in the course of revolution, the Moscow trials and purges, and the transformation of 'Asiatic barbarians . . . from illiterate, uncultured masses into an educated population.' The Cold War, Chinese Communism, and relations with the United States round out this picture. An important contribution."

—Horn Book

"This book is worth having. . . . Well done—it makes you stop and think, and perhaps discuss."

—Kirkus Reviews

Jules Archer
History for Young Readers

MAN OF STEEL:
JOSEPH STALIN

RUSSIA'S RUTHLESS RULER

JULES ARCHER

Foreword by Brianna DuMont

Sky Pony Press
NEW YORK

Historical texts often reflect the time period in which they were written, and new information is constantly being discovered. This book was originally published in 1965, and much has changed since then. While every effort has been made to bring this book up to date, it is important to consult multiple sources when doing research.

Sky Pony Press books may be purchased in bulk at special discounts for sales promotion, corporate gifts, fund-raising, or educational purposes. Special editions can also be created to specifications. For details, contact the Special Sales Department, Sky Pony Press, 307 West 36th Street, 11th Floor, New York, NY 10018 or info@skyhorsepublishing.com.

Sky Pony® is a registered trademark of Skyhorse Publishing, Inc.®, a Delaware corporation.

Visit our website at www.skyponypress.com.

10 9 8 7 6 5 4 3 2 1

Library of Congress Cataloging-in-Publication Data is available on file.

Print ISBN: 978-1-63450-177-4
Ebook ISBN: 978-1-5107-0702-3

Series design by Brian Peterson
Cover photo credit Associated Press

Printed in the United States of America

To
Eleanor Elsie Margaret with love, respect
and gratitude in that order

No giant of history has ever been so complex, so shrouded in mystery and contradiction, so baffling to understand, as Joseph Stalin. His biographers have had a difficult time sorting fact from legend because both his enemies and admirers, as well as Stalin himself, did not hesitate to distort events to suit their polemics. Some facts are impossible to pin down irrefutably because much of working-class life in pre-revolutionary Georgia went unrecorded. And not until Stalin was fifty did others who knew him try to recall in print his origins and beginnings. Stalin also deliberately destroyed many historical records and falsified others, even ordering the fakery of photographs, to burnish his image.

The biographer in search of the whole truth about Stalin must play literary detective, matching clues from all available evidence, evaluating each source for bias. I have tried to do just that in writing the fascinating life story of the incredible Russian who did more, perhaps, than any other single figure of the twentieth century to change the world we live in.

—Jules Archer

CONTENTS

Foreword

There's nothing better than a great villain in stories. Heroes can be so goody-goody and one-dimensional. Villains, on the other hand, have layers. Who doesn't feel a teeny bit bad for the Gollums and Lokis of the bad boy world? And who doesn't secretly love to watch the Joker at work? Admit it, you even rooted for the Wicked Witch of the West. Come on, Dorothy killed her sister! Jules Archer does one better for nonfiction. He personalizes one of the world's greatest villains of all time.

Joseph Stalin went by many names as serial fugitives usually do. Personally, he liked "Stalin" since it meant "man of steel." He certainly was steely. Like most villains, he had a sad backstory that contributed to his world view. Dirt was richer than his family. As Archer puts it, Stalin was born without any spoon, let alone a silver one. His alcoholic father beat him, and his perpetually sad mother worked her fingers to the bone as a laundress. These experiences made Stalin determined to hurt those who were lucky in birth, and the Russia-sized chip on his shoulder set the course for world history.

To Stalin, the ends justified the means, and that made him more terrifying than cannibalistic Hannibal Lector. Even in school, he was that scary kid who never had to actually fight to win an argument, because he used his wits and well-placed rumors to beat the other boys into submission.

By the time he was eighteen, he was a bona fide revolutionary who admired Karl Marx and Vladimir Lenin. Like all the best villains, he had more shades of gray than a paint store. Committed to Marxist principles, Stalin believed in the type of government where everything is shared and there are no aristocrats or peasants, called communism. In a nutshell, it meant the same healthcare, education, and food for all.

Stalin wasn't the type of politician who pretended to live frugally and then secretly ordered a cellar's worth of wine and dancing girls every night. He lived as simply as he preached. Archer shows us the honest side of Stalin as well as the dark ways he went about achieving his vision. And how he ended up betraying it, too.

Russia was living in the medieval past when the Bolsheviks (meaning "majority") tossed out the monarchy during the October Revolution of 1917. Stalin held different positions of influence within the party until Lenin's death in 1924 when he secured ultimate power. (Which, yes, is against Marxist principles where power is shared.) He crowned himself dictator for life, and he used secret police, mass killings, and pure terror to rule. All not nice things.

He wanted to lead the feudal lands into the industrial present with his "Five-Year Plans". The goal was to modernize—and fast—by building factories and churning out goods. He collectivized farms under government control in order to increase food production, which was then shared.

Unfortunately, it backfired. Workers were pushed beyond human limits, and the huge upheaval in farming led to massive famines. Anyone who resisted didn't survive, and that's not to mention the war against kulaks—farm owners. Stalin wanted to exterminate that entire class of people. The estimates for how many people died due to famine or firing squads vary wildly, but they can reach into the tens of millions.

Besides his bad habit of using mass graves as a political tool, Stalin wasn't a total monster all the time. Archer talks about the etiquette and dancing classes, education programs, arts, and scientific progress that flourished under him. For the first time, Russians read more Shakespeare than the English.

He championed, too, the little countries that wanted to declare their freedom. Unlike, as Archer points out, America whose "Let Freedom Ring" theme song didn't stop presidents from propping up crooked dictators around the world. These are all interesting shades of Stalin to pay attention to as you read Archer's book.

Throughout, keep in mind that Stalin's legacy is *still* complicated in modern-day Russia. Under him, technology advanced to the point where the Soviets achieved something incredible: they were the first to launch stuff into space, including a satellite, a man, and a dog. This spurred America to "go to the moon!" Would it have happened as quickly without this fierce competition?

In his author's note, Jules Archer says Stalin "did more, perhaps, than any other single figure of the twentieth century to change the world we live in." This fact was abundantly clear to Archer, who wrote this book during the capitalism vs. communism wars. But Stalin is still important to us today, and not just for the millions of people who live under communism.

While you read, think about the dangers of "utopia." What is given up to achieve a "perfect" society, and whose version of perfect wins? Does it seem like Marx's version, or even Lenin's version won? Do they have anything to do with how Stalin ruled the Soviet Union?

Although we live in a very different society than Stalin's Russia, we still grapple with questions that he tried to answer for his own people, such as the distribution of wealth, the question of class, and the role of the government in our economy. Should the government intervene to ensure that everyone has healthcare and that our wealth is distributed more equitably? Or, should the wealthy class—the so-called One Percenters—be allowed to keep a disproportionate share of the assets and power? What about things we take for granted, like Social Security which provides a critical safety net for the elderly? These are all questions that our society still struggles with today, and they are all things that Stalin advocated. He just went about them in brutal, inhuman ways.

In summing up Stalin, Archer quotes British MP, Herbert Morrison, who said Stalin was "a great man, but not a good man." Now it's time to decide for yourself.

—Brianna DuMont, 2017

I

Shoemaker's Son

He was born in a sagging hovel of Gori, a village of Georgia Province in the most southerly part of Russia, on December 21, 1879. His mother, Katherine Djugashvili, a twenty-one-year-old peasant, prayed desperately that he would not die after birth like her three previous babies. She christened him Joseph Vissarionovich ("son of Vissarion"), but the name tinder which he later shook the world was his revolutionary alias of Stalin ("man of steel").

His father, Vissarion Ivanovich Djugashvili, a gloomy man and a shoemaker by trade, had been born into serfdom. Vissarion had bitter memories of the semibarbaric feudal system which enslaved whole families to powerful, rich landowners. Viewed contemptuously as little better than animals, serfs were brutally beaten to make them work harder, kept at starvation level, tortured if desperation drove them to steal, taxed to support a medieval church, forced to watch their sons being dragged off to war by brutal conscription officers. Lucky serfs, it was said, died early and peacefully. Vissarion's father had been killed by a landowner's whip.

Tsar Alexander II had liberated the serfs in 1861, but ironically many found themselves worse off with no master committed to feed, clothe or shelter them. Opening a tiny shoemaking shop in Gori, Vissarion soon went bankrupt and had to take a job in a dingy shoe factory in nearby Tiflis.

Brooding over the wretchedness of his existence, Vissarion began to drink heavily. His wife Katherine was forced to take in washing and bake bread for prosperous Gori families, to earn back the rubles he squandered on wine and vodka. This humiliation only added to Vissarion's sense of guilt and defeat, and he took out his frustrations on his young son. Joseph was bewildered by the undeserved, savage beatings he suffered without warning. They filled him with hatred for his father and made him grim and heartless.

Katherine Djugashvili was a meek, long-suffering woman from the Caucasus Mountains region near the borders of Turkey and Iran. She bore all her trials without murmur, finding comfort in the Orthodox Church, the prevailing Christian religion of Russia and the eastern Mediterranean countries. Her hopes all centered in her son—nicknamed Sosso—for whom she cherished the dream that he would become a priest. In Tsarist Russia a family's social position was enhanced by having a priest in the family, and a priest, moreover, was immune from military service, taxation and the whip.

To compensate for her husband's drunken cruelty toward their son, she spoiled him, made excuses for his misbehaviour, patiently endured his dark rages of resentment.

The home of the Djugashvilis was a dismal shanty of cheap brick and timber, with two crude stone slabs for front steps, facing a rough cobblestone alley through which a malodorous stream trickled. Here young Sosso played until he was nine, when his drink-ravaged father died. Relatives insisted that Sosso must now take his father's place at the shoe factory in Tiflis as an apprentice, but Katherine Djugashvili would not hear of it. She begged the parish priest to obtain a scholarship for her son at the Gori Theological School, and he did.

To pay for his extra school expenses, she sewed long hours by candlelight when she was finished with her baking and laundry chores. Sosso's awareness of her sacrifices embittered him when he realized how easy it was for the middle class, or bourgeoisie, to send their sons to school.

The monk-taught Gori school, which faced the village's unpaved main street, harboured mostly sons of priests, petty officials and merchants. One morning in 1888, they scornfully observed the admission of the new pupil, a small, slim boy with a mop of black hair. His cheap school uniform testified to his lack of family status.

"You've made a mistake, fellow," one boy drawled. "This school is for gentry. They don't teach boot-mending here."

The other boys laughed, Sosso paled, clenched his fists and kept silent. But he stared at his tormentor with such unnerving ferocity, his almond-shaped eyes black with rage, that the other boy lowered his mocking gaze in embarrassment.

All through his stay at the Gori school, Sosso suffered from a humiliating sense of social inferiority. He refused to visit friends' homes, finding the difference between their circumstances and his own too embarrassing. He tried to compensate by becoming the best scholar in class, and by dominating every playtime escapade from hurling rocks to cliff-climbing.

To force others to accept his leadership, he devised cunning tactics such as studying their weaknesses, then mocking them so mercilessly that they sought his good graces to be spared. He managed to avoid fist fights by ridiculing antagonists for using violence as a substitute for brains. Few of his classmates dared balk at his commands. Once he jumped on another boy's back and rode him around the schoolyard, shouting jubilantly to schoolmates, "*Fa stal, ya stall!*" (I am steel!)

The rugged, spectacularly beautiful region in which he grew up was part of a world not fully emerged from the Middle Ages, where people still owed loyalty to tribes rather than provinces or nations. They lived in awe of feudal princes and a Byzantine church that glorified Middle East splendour. Gori was a country town on the banks of the Kura in a semi-tropical Georgian valley noted for wheat and wine; a crossroads where Asiatic peoples had spilled through into Europe. Sosso thrilled to tales of Alexander the Great and Genghis Khan, who had once fought in these fields. Sosso was constantly reminded that ancient Tartar blood ran in the veins of many Georgians, whenever he stared up at the two-thousand-year-old oriental fortress dominating the town from a hill.

Georgia had been annexed by Russia as a protectorate in 1783 to save it from Turkish aggression, but the Georgians had remained closer in spirit to Tartar than Russian culture. The diverse nationalities of Georgia—Georgians, Armenians, Turks, Kurds, Jews—lived at drawn daggers, hating each other even more than they hated the Russians who had formally swallowed them into the Tsarist Empire in 1803.

Like Sosso, most of his schoolmates were Georgian, speaking one of the seventy different languages of the Caucasus, all of them forbidden at school. They were forced to speak, read and learn in the Russian language only. In later years, when Sosso went north, his Georgian accent was ridiculed among "real" Russians—those who were oriented toward European culture, as opposed to those living under the influence of Asia Minor.

Another deep influence in young Sosso's life was the patriotic example of fierce, illiterate tribes of the towering Caucasus Mountains in fighting off every attempt by the Russians to change or pacify them. As a boy he often passed Kevsurs in the mountains—horsemen claiming to descend from the Crusaders, wearing coats of mail, buckles, armpieces; each man carrying a sabre, dagger, pistol and cartridge belt. They robbed other tribes more often than they fought their Russian oppressors, but Sosso saw them only as romantic heroes.

He and his best friend at school, Iremashvili, shared a deep passion for poems glorifying mountaineers who sacrificed their lives for the cause of Georgian Independence. They, too, yearned to join the struggle to win freedom from Russia. Sosso's face shone with pride and joy when he was able to persuade schoolmates to nickname him "Koba," after a folk hero he idolized. He preserved the name for many years, and it became his first alias as a revolutionist.

In 1891 and 1892, there was a serious famine in Georgia. Peasants were forced to return to their old masters as "voluntary serfs" to avoid starvation. Their anger was fed by a peasant political party called the Social Revolutionaries, who preached a brand of violent anarchy known as Populism, or Nihilism. Sosso became aware of their activities when bands of peasants raided, robbed, and burned the mansions of wealthy landowners around Gori.

He was only thirteen when curiosity led him to obtain and study some of the clandestine Populist pamphlets being circulated by the Social Revolutionaries. One pamphlet especially astonished him—an attack on the Orthodox Church. Scoffing at the Biblical interpretation of man as a miracle created by God, it explained Darwin's theory that man was a creature of evolution. Excited by his first exposure to scientific thought, Sosso managed to get hold of books by and about Darwin. That summer, leaving the village church after singing in the choir, he told one of the other choirboys smugly, "You know, they are deceiving us. There is no God. That's just empty chatter. Darwin says we are descended from apes, not from Adam."

"You're going to burn in hell!" the other boy gasped.

Sosso carefully concealed his heresy from his Gori teachers. They considered him such a model pupil that they helped him obtain a scholarship for the Tiflis Theological Seminary, a high school seventy versts (forty-six miles) from Gori. His hypocrisy didn't trouble him in the least. The seminary was his only chance for a higher education, and he was perfectly willing to endure the theology lessons for the sake of the academic courses. He had already decided that the ends justified the means, a conviction from which he was never to swerve.

Leaving sleepy little Gori behind, Sosso was fascinated by bustling Tiflis with its narrow, filthy, winding lanes crowded with camels, water carriers, donkeys laden with wineskins and pottery, pack mules carrying bright carpets from Kurdistan, sabre-clanking horsemen in Asiatic costume. Whenever he could escape from the seminary, he loved to wander along the labyrinth of Persian, Armenian, and Tartar bazaars, sharing the excitement of the colourful movement swirling around him, listening to the shrill cries of oriental traders, smelling the exotic scents of the southern lands.

There was excitement of a different kind at the seminary. For twenty years, the school had been a storm center because the all-Russian clerical faculty showed open scorn for Georgian nationalism, clashing constantly with the largely Georgian student body. In 1886 the Russian rector had been stabbed to death by a 19-year-old student for sneering at the Georgian language. Students called secret revolutionary meetings, joined by oil and railway workers of Tiflis, which was becoming the boom town now known as Tbilisi. A new rector confined students to the seminary day and night, and warned that they must have no further contact with the workers of Tiflis.

For mental and spiritual nourishment they were ordered to content themselves with religious lectures and endless prayers, and to compose long essays on topics like "In what language did Balaam's ass speak?" Enforcement of these dreary rules was placed in the hands of a sadistic school inspector named Abashidze, who spied on the students with great cunning.

But instead of studying for the priesthood, students ironically used the seminary to prepare for careers as revolutionaries. Sosso lost no time in following suit.

Strong-willed and brash, he did not take kindly to the harsh discipline, and enjoyed pitting his wits against the snooping tactics of Abashidze. None of the inspector's wiles could prevent Sosso's frequent escapes through a rear window and down a drainpipe to join some seminary students who had been expelled, and who were now secretly organizing a new revolutionary party in Tiflis.

They quickly appointed him their link with the student body in the seminary. On October 29, 1895, the secretly circulated Tiflis journal *Iberya* carried a defiant poem calling for Georgian independence under the byline of "Sosselo" (Little Joe). The sixteen-year-old revolutionist's first public utterance showed the influence of Shelley:

Know that the one who fell like ashes to the ground, Who long ago became enslaved. Will rise more high than these great crags Winged with brilliant hope.

Sosso's prestige soared among his fellow students, and went even higher as he began smuggling in forbidden books secured for him by his friends on the *Iberya*. These included works by Marx, Lenin, Tolstoy, Dostoyevsky, Gogol, Schopenhauer, Shelley, Chekhov, Hugo, Darwin—all banned to students because they contained provocative thoughts not considered in the best interests of Church, Tsar or hereditary nobility.

The smuggled books were passed around for surreptitious reading at chapel and in dormitories, where they were secretly pored over by candlelight. No one read more indefatigably than the determined "booklegger" himself, who even managed to read a book under the table while eating. On cold, damp nights, he would read into the small hours until he began to cough, waking Iremashvili, who would remove his books and snuff his candle, ignoring his whispered protests.

While Sosso immersed himself clandestinely in the great thoughts of his century, certain Russian events outside the seminary were shaping his future. At that time the Tsarist government operated under an economic system best described as "unfree enterprise." A ruling group of rich noblemen, merchants, and landowners ran Russia for their own benefit, monopolizing the wealth, enjoying all the privileges, controlling all the political power. They were subsidized and supported by the Tsar but were in turn his sources of power, along with the army and the Holy Synod, or high Church council. Russia was run like a vast bureaucracy, with peasants ruled by police, police by county officials, and so on up to the Tsar.

Sosso's books taught him that this whole structure, as well as the capitalist system of Western democracies, was being challenged and threatened by the German revolutionists Karl Marx and Friedrich Engels. In a historic pamphlet called *The Communist Manifesto,* Marx predicted that capitalism would be swept aside in a worldwide revolt of the working classes, to be replaced by a new classless society called Communism, under which workers would receive all the benefits of their own labour by owning and operating everything communally. The Communist slogan was "Workers of the world, unite! You have nothing to lose but your chains!" Marx aimed all his efforts at the factory workers of Western Europe, especially Germany, convinced that revolution would come first to the highly industrialized nations, and last to a backward, sprawling feudal society like Russia.

But it was in Russia that his ideas excited the greatest revolutionary fervour, because the peasants and workers under the Tsar were desperate for change, *any* change. The Social Revolutionaries, who led terrorist raids against the hated landowners, were determined that the Russian peasants would lead the nation to Marxism. But in 1898, a rival Marxist party was formed in Minsk. Calling themselves Social Democrats, they secretly swore to overthrow the Tsar and establish Communism through rule by factory workers. Sosso was permitted to join them when he was eighteen. To win other converts for the Party, he organized a secret "seminary within the seminary," turning theology study lessons into clandestine readings and discussions of Marxist theory. Students who dared challenge his opinion usually withered under his biting sarcasm. Those who didn't, felt his wrath in the malicious gossip he spread about them.

Inspector Abashidze's raids to discover forbidden books left Sosso disdainful. He was reported to the rector no less than thirteen times for this offence, each time being locked in a narrow, windowless punishment cell to do a day's penance for his sin. He was proud of this persecution. By 1899, his disinterest in keeping up even a pretence of theological studies was so obvious that his grades slipped from best to worst in his class. When his teachers reproached him, he simply regarded them with a contemptuous smile. Four months before graduation, the rector finally expelled him.

Five years of grim seminary life did not fail to leave their mark on Sosso. They hardened him for the stony, wretched life of a professional revolutionary. They taught him religious fanaticism, and he applied it to Communism. Inspector Abashidze's spy system was the inspiration for his own secret police, which he used years later to suppress dangerous thoughts. He never scorned to learn from and imitate his enemies.

In 1900, he took a meagrely paid post as clerk at the Tiflis Observatory. The job gave him some money to live on and masked his real work of agitating among the railway workers of Tiflis. Now, hoping to disguise his youth with a sparse beard, he moved among them in a black peasant blouse and red necktie, his black hair an uncombed bramble jutting from beneath a slanted, flat Russian peak cap.

The Tiflis workers admired the young radical with the rough, sarcastic wit. He impressed them by his indifference to food, cold, and comfort, his hard common sense, his knowledge of forbidden books, his dogged devotion to revolutionary ideals. They began calling him "our Sosso," chuckling when he slyly mocked a Social Revolutionary. "I can't imagine why the workers want to listen to people as unimportant as us," he would deride a rival, "when they have you fine fellows to lead them!" To give his shrewd mind ample time for second thoughts, he taught himself to speak slowly and cautiously, selecting words that struck at the heart of a matter or of an opponent.

Energetic, resourceful, resolute, he was only twenty-one when he won election to the Tiflis executive committee of the Party. He helped plan the first May Day demonstration in the Caucasus, a bold working-class challenge to Tsarist power. The plotters hoped it would inspire thousands of Georgian workers to flock to the Red banner, flag of international revolution, and impress European comrades that the Social Democrats, not the Social Revolutionaries, were the true Marxist force in Russia.

On May 1, 1900, young Sosso proudly led five hundred railway workers with Red banners and portraits of Marx and Engels in a demonstration on the outskirts of Tiflis.

Joseph Djugashvili was on his way.

2

The Young Terrorist

The May Day marchers halted in a cobblestone square, forming a circle around their youthful leader. As soon as he began to speak, Cossacks and *Okhrana* (political police) suddenly galloped up, charging their horses into the crowd. Workers fled before their flailing whips and slashing sabres.

But by May Day one year later, the Social Democrats had grown strong enough to challenge Tsarist authority in the very heart of Tiflis, this time with a demonstration by two thousand workers. Again there was a bloody clash, but now in addition to the wounds of the workers there were also heads broken among the Tsar's forces. Stalin felt proud when the Party's newspaper, *Iskra (The Spark),* declared, "The event is of historical importance—a day that marked the beginning of an open revolutionary movement in the Caucasus."

The editor of *Iskra* was Vladimir Ilyich Lenin, a small bearded revolutionist who was one of the chief founders of the Social Democratic Party. Young Stalin stood in awe of his reputation in much the same way a patriot leader of the Boston Tea Party might have looked up to Samuel Adams or Tom Paine.

Lenin had just finished serving three years of exile in Siberia and was editing *Iskra* from abroad, smuggling it into Russia. He hoped to make the paper a uniting force among all Marxist groups, rallying them to the banner of the Social Democrats. By 1901, the revolutionary movement was growing fast, but it was too fragmented by splinter groups, each too weak alone to cause Tsar Nicholas serious worry. The Social Revolutionaries were still the largest Marxist party. Their strength, however, lay in the country rather than in the cities.

In Tiflis, Stalin was both agitator and educator. He organized secret meetings in workers' homes, teaching unschooled railwaymen why revolution was "inevitable." He explained that during the last decades of the nineteenth century, the Industrial Revolution had reshaped the lives of hundreds of millions of Europeans and Americans who now worked in large factories controlled by a small number of industrialists. These business owners, supported and protected by their governments, viewed labour as simply another operating cost, to be bought as cheaply as possible for maximum profits. In 1901, this meant fourteen-hour workdays, low wages, sordid working conditions.

The same "robber baron" philosophy prevailed in agriculture; wealthy landowners lived affluently on the hard toil of peasants and sharecroppers, who were miserably paid and badly treated. In effect, Stalin argued, most common people of the Western world felt economically enslaved and so were ready for Marxist leaders to help them overthrow the capitalists.

He warned workers against the Social Revolutionaries who wasted working-class anger in senseless assassinations and led bands of peasants to raid, rob and burn the mansions of landowners. Lenin, whose older brother had been hanged as a Populist terrorist, had told his disciples, "We must follow a different path. Bomb-throwing is *not* the true path for revolutionists." The true path, Stalin urged, was the tight discipline of the Social Democratic Party, which knew how to direct the exploited and oppressed in seizing power. Shrewdly aware of the emotional impact of words like "exploited" and "oppressed," Stalin used them freely.

His tireless agitation did not escape the vigilance of the Okhrana, who broke into his empty room at the Tiflis Observatory to arrest him in the spring of 1901. He promptly fled into hiding, beginning an outlaw's life which lasted sixteen years. Elusive as an eel, he vanished as Joseph Djugashvili but reappeared with forged passports as Ivanovich, David, Kato, Ryaboi, Vassilyev, Chizhikov, Nizheradze, Koba—especially as Koba, his boyhood hero—and finally as Stalin.

The Okhrana sought him everywhere, but he became an artist at slipping through their fingers. Penniless, indifferent to hardship, he was fed and hidden by admiring Party comrades. At secret meetings, he suddenly materialized out of the night, spoke swiftly as a worker watched for police at the window, then melted away as mysteriously as he had appeared.

One night, a police spy tipped off the Okhrana that he was meeting with fellow conspirators in a building connected to the Tiflis theatre. Jubilant police quickly surrounded the building and broke in, only to find it empty. Stalin had kicked open the connecting door to the theatre, then scattered with his comrades into the audience, where they immediately began watching the show with absorbed expressions.

Stalin had the same steel faith in the coming of Communism that the early Roman martyrs had in the ultimate triumph of Christianity, and *Iskra* was his revolutionary Bible. He was inspired by Lenin's glorification of the Party's hunted, ragged, idealistic, full-time agitators as the hope of Russia.

"We must educate men," Lenin wrote, "who devote to the revolution not only their free evenings, but their whole lives." Stalin took deep pride in his role as a professional revolutionary. He felt grateful to Lenin for having filled his life with great purpose; for having made the Party organizer a heroic figure among his fellow men.

In November, 1901, Stalin was elevated to the nine-man Tiflis committee directing Party activity in the Caucasus. In their illegal Georgian-language paper called *Brdzola (The Struggle),* he wrote melodramatically: "Not only the working class has been groaning under the yoke of Tsardom. Groaning is the hunger-swollen Russian peasantry. . . . Groaning, too, are the lower middle class under the Tsarist knout and bludgeon, especially the educated . . . the oppressed Russian nationalities and religions . . . the endlessly persecuted and humiliated Jews . . . the Georgians and Armenians denied their own schools and State jobs."

The Party sent him to Batum, an important oil centre near the Turkish border on the shores of the Black Sea. Setting up a small portable hand press, he began flooding the Rothschild and Matascheff oil works with incendiary leaflets. Once, with the police hot on their heels, Stalin and a comrade fled carrying dismantled parts of the press. They hid in a field of corn, listening to the shouts, cries, and galloping hooves of the hunt swirling around them. Stalin suddenly became aware that they were being observed impassively by a white-bearded Moslem standing a few feet away. He implored the peasant not to betray them to their pursuers.

"I am the most insignificant, most persecuted of men," the Moslem replied quietly. "What reason would I have to love or serve the Okhrana? Besides, while I have never spoken to the chief of the Batum revolutionists, I would be a fool, indeed, not to recognize him. Welcome to the poor farm of Khashim, son of thunder and lightning. Allah bless thy great heart!"

Marxist leaflets were soon leaving Khashim's farmhouse beneath the voluminous dresses of radicals disguised as Moslem women, their faces hidden behind long *chadras* veils. Turbaned Khashim himself sold fruits and vegetables at factory gates, wrapping his wares in Red tracts concealed at the bottom of the basket. His neighbours, suspicious of the clanking noises in his house, gossiped that Khashim was harbouring a ring of counterfeiters. A group of Moslems came to see Stalin, demanding a share in the illicit enterprise.

"I'm not printing rubles," he explained. "Just tracts that tell why the poor workers and peasants don't have any."

The villagers were surprised but impressed. "This is even better," their spokesman said. "We will circulate these for you for nothing. But to prove that we can trust you, you must promise to embrace the Moslem faith."

Stalin cheerfully agreed, always ready to make any cynical promise that would advance the cause of the Revolution.

The Okhrana failed to discover the press. Some sixteen years later when the Red flag flew over the Kremlin, the son of Khashim hit something hard while digging in their garden, and pulled up a rusted hand press. He asked his aged father what it was. "With the crop from that, my son," Khashim quavered proudly, "we helped Comrade Stalin make the Revolution."

On April 5, 1902, the Okhrana succeeded at last in trapping the wily Koba, as he was then known, at a Party meeting in Batum. He was flung into prison to await trial, an incarceration that dragged on for a whole year and a half.

Calmly accepting this setback, Stalin viewed prison as simply another place in which to recruit converts to the Party. He rose early each morning, exercised briskly, studied German economics for a better understanding of Marx, then engaged other prisoners in debate. His shrewd logic, seasoned with deadly scorn, was usually triumphant. He also inspired the prisoners to protest jail conditions by shouting, whistling, breaking dishes and furniture, and banging boots on cell doors.

Proof of the Party's esteem for him came in March, 1903. The steel-willed prisoner was notified he had been elected to the executive board of the new All-Caucasian Federation of Social Democrats. But five months later he was stunned by news that the cause for which he was in jail had suddenly split in half.

At the Second Party Congress in London, a fierce fight had broken out between the Party's moderate and radical wings.

His idol Lenin led the radical Bolsheviks (meaning "majority"), insisting that the Party must remain a small, elite band of professional revolutionaries. They must wage class warfare without compromise, always leading the masses, never being led by them. The Mensheviks ("minority"), led by intellectual Yuri Martov, wanted a large, democratically run party willing to accept gradual reforms for the benefit of *all* Russia—not just the proletariat, or working class. This battle split the Party wide open, and Lenin resigned from *Iskra* to head the new Bolshevik faction. Stalin promptly pledged his allegiance from jail.

In November, 1903, the Batum court finally put him on trial. Labelled a politically dangerous criminal, he was sentenced to Siberia for three years of "administrative exile."

Now wearing a thick black mustache, the cynical-eyed, young Bolshevik joined fifteen other deportees on a freezing, month-long journey to the tiny snowbound village of Novaya Uda in Irkutsk Province. Here, despite his iron constitution, his health began to suffer from meagre rations and the Siberian winter, and he developed a tubercular cough. The outbreak of the Russo-Japanese war early in 1904 gave him hope of escape. Expanding eastward along its new Trans-Siberian Railway, Russia had made Manchuria a virtual protectorate, and the Tsar was now eager to grab Korea. The alarmed Japanese decided to strike without warning. Their naval attack against Port Arthur in the Yellow Sea created such excitement and confusion in Russia that little attention was paid to guarding exiles in Siberia. The revolutionary underground was quick to take advantage by organizing escape routes.

Stalin slipped out of Novaya Uda alone on January 5th and headed south on foot across the open steppes, or woodless plains, of the Kuznetsk Basin. Following a frozen river, he was suddenly overwhelmed by a terrible ice blizzard that could kill anyone caught in the open. It took him two hours and all his strength to battle his way through the storm a mile and a half to the nearest hut on the escape route. By the time he staggered into it, he was a frightening apparition of moving ice. Thawed out in front of a log fire, he collapsed and slept through an entire day. When he awoke he was frostbitten, but his cough had disappeared, the merciless Siberian winter ironically curing when it failed to kill.

By early February he was back in the Tiflis underground leading the Georgian struggle against the Mensheviks, who exerted far more influence in Tiflis than the Bolsheviks. The Mensheviks, pointing out wryly that he spent more energy in fighting them than the Tsar, called him "the most hated of the Caucasian Bolsheviks." Stalin was joined in this battle by Leon Kamenev, a young Bolshevik who had been one of Lenin's personal lieutenants abroad. Stalin listened to Kamenev's proud reminiscences about their idol with a mixture of awe and envy.

Hidden in the obscurity of Stalin's early years as a revolutionist is his courtship of and marriage to a tall, dark, illiterate Tiflis girl, Katherine Svanidze, who presented him with a son, Jacob. She saw little of her fugitive husband, who was far too busy working for the Revolution—when not in jail, exile, or flight from the Okhrana—to devote precious hours to such un-Bolshevik concerns as a wife and son.

"Comrade Koba had neither home nor family," recalled one of his followers. "He lived and thought exclusively for the Revolution." This may have been one reason why Jacob Djugashvili, backward in school and neglected, forever bore deep resentment against the father who had had no time for his son.

A general strike of Baku oil workers broke out in the summer of 1904. When it faltered, Stalin was rushed to Baku by the Party to provide Bolshevik leadership. He ordered a huge demonstration in front of the mosque of a Moslem worker who had been shot by the police. The nervous Baku chief of police forbade this, so Stalin decided instead that a choir of workers singing revolutionary dirges would accompany the funeral procession. The police chief roared angrily that radical sentiments must not be sung. Stalin's splendid mustache curved in a frosty smile, and he ordered the workers just to whistle the tune.

"Everyone knows the words anyhow," he chuckled.

His leadership of the Baku strike compelled the oil industrialists to sign the first collective agreement ever signed in Russia. One police agent sourly reported, "The strike leader, Kaisom Nijeradze, revived the morale of disheartened workers through agitation and illegal literature." But the Okhrana failed to identify Nijeradze as the escaped Siberian exile Koba.

Labour unrest soared with the fall of Port Arthur in January, 1905, and the Tsar's humiliating defeat in the Russo-Japanese War. A general strike paralyzed St. Petersburg, capital of Russia.

Elated, Stalin was convinced that the time had come for the long-awaited Revolution. The disillusioned Tsarist Army, in weary retreat from Siberia, was in no mood to fight Russian workers to prop up a bungling, oppressive aristocracy.

On January 21st, Stalin issued a fiery proclamation in the name of the Caucasian Union of Social Democrats: "Workers of the Caucasus, the hour of revenge has struck! The Tsarist autocracy is losing its main support—its warriors. It will try to bribe you with a few concessions, but the time has come to destroy the Tsarist Government, and destroy it we shall! Russia is like a loaded gun at full cock, ready to go off at the slightest concussion. Let us therefore join hands and rally around the Party Committees. Only they can lead us in a worthy manner—only they can light the way for us to the Promised Land—our Marxist world!"

Even now his seminary training impelled him to use a Biblical parallel to urge revolution. Paradoxically, too, the St. Petersburg strike was being led by a unique Orthodox priest, Father Gapon, who held Menshevik views. The day after Stalin's appeal, Gapon led a procession of two hundred thousand men, women and children in the snow, carrying ikons and portraits of the Tsar, singing "God Bless the Tsar." Carrying a petition for an eight-hour day, a minimum wage of one ruble (about twenty pence) a day, and representative government, Gapon led the procession to the gates of the Tsar's Winter Palace. The nervous Palace Guard opened fire, killing five hundred and wounding several thousand more. The red snow of St. Petersburg on "Bloody Sunday" outraged the Russian people.

Stalin and other Bolshevik leaders lost no time in capitalizing on the massacre. The country was swept with strikes, demonstrations and wild disorders. On February 17th, the Governor of Moscow, Grand Duke Serge Alexandrovich, was assassinated. Before the year was over, fifteen hundred Tsarist officials were killed, and many cities saw armed risings of workers.

Ministers of the frightened Tsar urged him to stave off revolution by dividing his enemies, turning one against the other, counting on old national hatreds to prevent popular unity. So the government swiftly and secretly organized black-masked gangs called the Black Hundreds to spread counter terror, diverting the anger of the masses against scapegoat minority groups like Jews, intellectuals, and radicals. In the Caucasus these gangs incited Armenian and Turkish children to fight each other; killed Turks, then Armenians, by turn from ambush; then alternately burned the homes of each. Full-scale civil war broke out between the two ancient enemies. The Black Hundreds also set fire to Baku factories and oil wells, spreading rumours to blame the strikers, whom they then hunted down and murdered.

Stalin pleaded desperately with his fellow Caucasians not to be diverted from carrying through the Revolution. In a tract called *Party Differences* he urged Mensheviks to forget their grievances against the Bolsheviks and join in a common fight against the Black Hundreds. The Mensheviks, more numerous and powerful than Lenin's followers in the Caucasus, spurned these overtures. It was some consolation to Stalin, however, to learn that Lenin himself had read and praised his pamphlet.

He decided to fight fire with fire. Organizing raids on private and government stores of arms, he set up secret Marxist depots to arm workers. His guerrilla squads scored victories against the Black Hundreds and helped stop tribal feuds.

The chaotic, uncoordinated Revolution of 1905 raged on spasmodically like a forest fire that, beaten out in one spot, flared up in another. In autumn the workers of St. Petersburg gave Tsar Nicholas a fresh shock. Led by Leon Trotsky, a brilliant young Menshevik, they held elections in the city's factories and shops, setting up the Petersburg Soviet (council) of Workers' Deputies. This new "government" proceeded to ignore the Tsar's decrees and started passing its own laws.

The nervous Tsar immediately agreed to permit elections for a national *Duma* (parliament), after first receiving assurances from his ministers that it would be dominated by hand-picked "safe" moderates, and its powers carefully limited. The Bolsheviks were wrathful when many Menshevik leaders voiced support for the Duma, The Bolsheviks urged an election boycott.

"Only on the bones of the oppressors," Stalin warned workers in the Caucasus, "can the people's freedom be founded!"

In October, a general strike spread from St. Petersburg to Moscow, then to all of Russia. It burgeoned into a full-scale revolution led by Trotsky, who considered himself a third force halfway between the rigid positions of Mensheviks and Bolsheviks. The revolution failed ingloriously, however, when he and other leaders of his faction were suddenly arrested and banished to Siberia. A new wave of strikes exploded in protest, and wild street battles broke out in Moscow.

Bolshevik leaders from all over Russia were hastily summoned to a national conference on December 24th at Tammerfors, Finland, then an autonomous province of the Tsarist Empire and safe for revolutionists. Stalin hurried north from the Caucasus, stirred by excited anticipation. For the first time he was going to move among the national leaders of the Party.

With luck he might even get a chance to meet the great man who had inspired his whole life as a revolutionary—Vladimir Ilyich Lenin!

3

Gathering Storm

Stalin had visualized his idol as a physical as well as mental giant. "I had hoped to see the mountain eagle of our Party," he wrote later. He was disappointed when Lenin turned out to be a small, plump, balding, ordinary-looking man in a cheap and baggy suit, looking more like a nervous grocer than a revolutionary mastermind. A typical Russian intellectual, Lenin was the rebellious, well-educated son of a middle-class bureaucrat. Stalin's chagrin vanished, however, when he heard his hero speak; Lenin's cold, brilliant logic overwhelmed him.

In turn, Lenin was impressed by his first meeting with the rough-mannered, moody, restless Georgian with Asiatic eyes. Stalin struck him as an earthy man of action, chary of words because of an embarrassing Caucasian peasant's accent. When the conference ended, he indicated his interest in Stalin by inviting him along with a few other favored delegates for revolver practice in the woods nearby. Stalin was enraptured.

In Russia, meanwhile, uncoordinated uprisings raged all through January, 1906. In Petersburg no papers appeared, no streetcars ran, no mail was delivered, no bread was baked, every factory was closed, crowds poured through the streets with Red banners. In the country, peasants burned and looted farmhouses, while Cossacks struck back with brutal pogroms against the Jews, whom anti-Semitic authorities blamed for stirring insurrection. Moscow workers fought the army for nine days from behind street barricades, but were finally driven off by artillery fire. By the time Stalin returned from Finland, the Tsar had already snuffed out local insurrections, one by one, his forces killing over fourteen thousand workers, wounding twenty thousand, arresting seventy thousand and executing over a thousand.

"No one is to be acquitted," Nicholas II ordered grimly. "And do not ask me to show mercy to anyone!" In the next three years two hundred thousand political prisoners were arrested, and the Black Hundreds shot down suspected radicals on sight.

Georgi Plekhanov, then leader of the Mensheviks, sighed in discouragement, "We should not have taken up arms."

The Mensheviks, who had taken control of the Social Democratic Party at a Stockholm congress in 1906, looked longingly west to Europe, especially Germany, where the Marxist movement was thriving. Known there as the Second International, its leaders advocated gradual reform of capitalism by ballot rather than its overthrow by bullet. With powerful working-class support they now controlled trade unions, published influential newspapers, elected their own representatives to public office. Lenin and the Bolsheviks, however, considered the Second International a betrayal of Marx's revolutionary teachings.

Socialism and Communism were at first loose terms used to describe any economic system which took the means of production out of private hands, and turned them over to the government for public operation. Gradually, however, Socialism came to stand for the Second International, or those pledged to defeat capitalism by peaceful means. Communism came to represent the violent overthrow of capitalism, and the seizing of power by Party leaders who would then rule as an elite "dictatorship of the proletariat."

The Bolsheviks, however, had their own rigid definitions of Socialism and Communism, based on the teachings of Marx. Socialism, they said, was the first lower stage of a revolutionary society which would pay workers each according to his ability.

Socialism would gradually give way to Communism, under which the state would wither away as unnecessary, and workers would then share the wealth each according to his need. No Bolshevik leader claimed to understand how Communism would work out in practice, but all insisted it was historically inevitable. Even today the Soviet Union regards itself simply as a Socialist state in transition toward the distant and misty dream of pure Communism.

In 1906 Stalin's thorniest problem was winning over Russia's rebellious minorities to a cause which, however Marxist, was still Russian. In Poland, then a Russian province, the Bolsheviks, carrying Red flags, attended a mass burial of Polish victims of the Revolution. The Polish Social Democrats, however, showed up with Polish flags. There was a fierce battle in which each group tore flags from the other's hands.

"I am a Marxist and a revolutionary," said a bitter Pole whose sister had been slashed across the face by a mounted Cossack's *nagaika* (whip). "But if any Russian tells me that those dirty Cossacks are *my* comrades and brothers, I say No, and No, and No! Russians have used their *nagaikas* too often in this country for Poles to wish them anything but dead!"

The bleak times on which the revolutionary movement had fallen were made even more dismal for Stalin when his wife died of pneumonia in 1907. Although revolutionary work had kept him away from Katherine most of the time, she had always welcomed him home tenderly, without complaint or reproach. He was so distraught at losing her that he numbly let her parents bury her with full Orthodox rites.

"Until I knew her I had a heart of stone," he said sadly to his boyhood friend Iremashvili at the grave. "Well, now that she's died, so have my last warm feelings for all human beings!"

As they left the cemetery, he informed his wife's parents that they were welcome to custody of his motherless two-year-old son Jacob, and could bring him up as their own.

He withdrew from all his old friends, including Iremashvili, and became increasingly cold, sarcastic, suspicious and vengeful. His one obsession became saving the Party, which was now in desperate need of funds. Stalin grimly decided that the time was long past for holier-than-thou denunciations of the Social Revolutionaries for their acts of terrorism. Why not use *their* tactics to raise money for Lenin?

It was a natural enough idea for anyone from the Caucasus, where robber bands lived on the fruits of banditry and were regarded as folk heroes for attacking Tsarist strongholds. Stalin's decision to turn criminal for his cause was not too different from the motivations of the "resistance" movement years later in sabotaging a Nazi-occupied Europe.

He organized fighting squads of Georgians into *boyeviki* (armed guerrillas) who threw bombs, attacked police, held up banks, post offices, trains, coaches and arsenals. Lenin, who had fled abroad to direct the Party in exile, welcomed the funds Stalin's bandits made available. Because police were constantly searching for him, Stalin had to stay in the background, conducting his terrorism through committees. This caution was not for want of any personal courage, which he had demonstrated on many occasions. Stalin genuinely felt that it was better for the Revolution if he lived for it rather than died for it.

Both Stalin and Lenin felt that the failure of the 1905 Revolution had been partly due to the Menshevik aversion to cruelty and bloodshed. Only by sacrificing individual human life as ruthlessly as the Tsar's forces did, they were convinced, could a new society be built that would be humane to the great mass of workers and peasants. "It is harder to kill a child than a Cossack," Stalin declared, "but a true Bolshevik will accept responsibility for killing that child if its death is necessary for the Revolution. Our concern must be for the happiness of generations of children not yet born."

Asked about the four thousand Russian victims of class warfare murdered by the *boyeviki* during 1906 and 1907, Stalin shrugged. "You cannot make a revolution with silk gloves," he said.

In May, 1907, he went to London under the alias "Ivanovich" to attend a Social Democratic Congress. He listened ironically as the eloquent Menshevik leader Leon Trotsky, just escaped from Siberian exile, poured withering scorn on Lenin and his Bolsheviks for hurting the prestige of the revolutionary movement by criminal activity and illegal expropriation of funds. The Congress obediently passed a resolution condemning all outlaw activity by Party members.

Lenin decided the Bolsheviks were now solvent enough to disband the *boyeviki,* so he sent Stalin to organize the oilfield workers of Baku on the Persian border, where ancient mosques and minarets were now becoming dwarfed by oil derricks. The illiterate Turkish, Persian, Armenian, and Russian workers gathered in thousands to hear Stalin harangue them as he clung to the upper portion of a street lamp. They were angry about being exploited by the European-owned oil companies, which paid them in *baksheesh* (tips) instead of wages, and even refused to let them marry without company permission.

"In the storm of conflict between workers and oil industrialists," Stalin wrote later of this period, "I first learned what it meant to lead big masses of workers."

He became convinced that the workers of Baku could not free themselves from the Asiatic practices of their employers because the Mensheviks had organized them into craft unions, each too weak to force concessions. He succeeded in bringing together all of Baku's shop and oilfield workers into one powerful industrial union, which then bargained with the entire oil industry.

Despite Stalin's success in Baku, he made many enemies among fellow Bolsheviks who resented his crafty maneuvers within Party ranks. With sly cunning, always working anonymously behind the scenes, he turned comrade against comrade to prevent support for any leader except himself. A few who realized what he was up to upbraided him as a "madman" and "disorganized." When his chief Party rival, a comrade named Shaumian, was arrested by Baku police, some Bolsheviks angrily suspected that it was Stalin himself who had denounced him.

After nine months of oilfield agitation, Stalin was arrested and held in a Baku prison awaiting exile again to Siberia. His revolutionary steel was tempered further by the miserable conditions and police brutality he now experienced. With fifteen hundred inmates crowded into a prison meant for four hundred, Stalin slept on a stairway. Even this miserable rest was often disturbed, as prisoners around him were suddenly snatched up in the middle of the night and dragged to a prison yard gallows.

Political prisoners were sometimes forced to walk through a gauntlet of soldiers who beat them with the butt ends of their guns. When it was Stalin's turn, he went through calmly with a book in his hand, studying Esperanto, which he believed would become the international language of the working class. He impressed other prisoners by his total indifference to pain.

For his closest companions in jail he chose men of action, his term for robbers, forgers, murderers, blackmailers, and other hardened criminals. Since committing all their crimes in the name of the Revolution, he had become impressed with men who knew how to "do and outdo."

He also sharpened his skill at intrigue. When one young workman angered him into a black mood, Stalin tipped off a fellow Bolshevik prisoner known as Mitka that the youth was a police spy, and should be eliminated quickly for the safety of all. Mitka promptly stabbed the youth to death. A fellow prisoner later described Stalin as "completely lacking principles, sly and exceptionally cruel."

Between 1908 and 1912, Stalin was arrested and exiled to Siberia five times, but managed to escape four times to continue agitating in Baku. Because of the ease with which he seemed able to escape, and his talent for survival, some Mensheviks suspected him of having made a secret deal to serve as police informer. The Okhrana used many turncoat *agents provocateurs,* among radicals both inside prison and out. But Stalin's prison file reveals only that the police saw him as "rude, impudent, disrespectful to superiors."

Constantly hunted, always operating under an alias, he was invaluable to the Bolsheviks as a relentless organizer who knew how to use the coarse speech of the illiterate railwaymen, tobacco pickers and oil workers of the Caucasus. It was really Stalin who held together the Bolshevik faction by his fanaticism in the bitter, hard years after 1906. An old comrade later recalled, "When our nerves were bad, when we lacked sleep and food, when things looked very black indeed, Stalin was always completely cool, like an icicle. Often in times of the severest stress he would suddenly say something very funny which relieved the tension. We all of us thought that Stalin was crude, even a crude joker. But when the crisis was over, we realized that Stalin's joke had been a deliberate psychological hypodermic. After a while we came to appreciate him."

Stalin's hardest struggles were to win workers away from the Mensheviks, who were popular for advocating Georgia's secession from Russia. He attacked this tactic as betraying the class struggle in favour of narrow nationalism, but when he dared debate the issue with better-educated Menshevik leaders, he was made to seem foolishly tongue-tied. Dark with rage, he told comrades, "All means are justified against Mensheviks!"

He was released from a fifth exile under strict orders to keep out of the Caucasus for five years. In January, 1912, he went to Prague for a Bolshevik conference called by Lenin to plan for an open break with the Mensheviks. Lenin planned to direct the Bolsheviks from exile, through a new four-man underground

Russian Bureau. To Stalin's great joy, Lenin named him one of the tetrarchy, who would also edit a new illegal Bolshevik newspaper called *Pravda*.

Early in 1913, Stalin went to Vienna for a Social Democratic Congress, hoping to win powerful supporters for Lenin's newly planned independent Bolshevik Party. He sought out Leon Trotsky, the vain, flamboyant but brilliant "third force" who had headed the Petersburg Soviet and the 1905 Revolution, and whom Stalin had only known until then by reputation. When he tried to strike up a conversation, Trotsky winced at the Georgian's coarse laughter and broken Russian. He turned his back coldly on the man he described later as "unendurably vulgar." Stalin's eyes glinted with animosity. Stung by Trotsky's snub, which had awakened his childhood feelings of social inferiority, he felt fresh rage against well-bred, middle-class Party intellectuals. Rising to speak at the Congress, he lashed out at Trotsky's proposals for reconciling Bolshevik and Menshevik differences as childish, and sneered at Trotsky as a common noisy champion with faked muscles.

In Vienna, he found that Lenin wanted his help in selling a thorny Bolshevik policy. Making up what Trotsky called "the Tsarist empire, that prison of nations," were Poles, Lithuanians, Ukrainians, Latvians, Estonians, Tartars, Jews, Georgians, Cossacks, Turkmen, Uzbecks and Armenians. Mensheviks wanted workers of each group to co-operate with their enemies, landowners and factory owners, to throw off Russian rule. Lenin wanted only workers to join forces to overthrow *all* Tsarist ruling groups in a class struggle. He asked Stalin to write a treatise which would convince Russia's workers of all nationalities why the Revolution had to come before all regional patriotic feeling.

In a forty-page signed analysis, *Marxism and the Nationalities Problem*, Stalin suppressed his own Georgian loyalties and wryly wrote that what each nationality really wanted was not equal rights but domination over the others. Self-determination for each would be possible only when international solidarity of the working class overthrew the Tsar. But even after the Revolution, he explained, no nationality would have reason to leave a new "Russian Federation" which would swiftly rectify and adjust all grievances. This shrewd paper solution of a complex problem won Stalin Lenin's praise as a "remarkable Georgian," and later led to his selection as Commissar of Nationalities.

Returning from Vienna to Petersburg, he hid from the Okhrana in the home of Serge Alliluyev, a Bolshevik workman. From this hideout he made contact with Roman Malinovsky, an eloquent Duma deputy who was one of Lenin's most trusted secret aides. Unknown to Lenin and Stalin, Malinovsky was a double agent for the Okhrana. He persuaded Stalin to attend a musical soiree given one night by the Party. When Tsarist police suddenly broke in, Stalin's comrades tried to smuggle him out of the house in a woman's coat, but the ruse failed.

This time he was exiled to remote Kureika, fifty miles north of the Arctic Circle, from which escape was impossible. In this ice-bound wilderness, winter was nine months long and the only cultural diversion consisted of books and papers sent by friends, delivered by dogsled two or three times a year. Stalin received parcels of food, clothing and books from the Alliluyev family, who had hidden him in Petersburg.

He led a hermit's existence for the most part, shunning the endless political debates around the samovar. Living in the frozen tundra like a Siberian Robinson Crusoe, he shot bears, wolves, and ptarmigan, caught fish through the ice, trapped rabbits and foxes. Eating well while others perished, the resourceful Bolshevik also kept himself warm in animal skins and furs. During infrequent visits to a friend, he would sit silent and morose for half an hour, then jump up and say, "Well, I have to go, goodbye." Political talk in the monotony of exile, he felt, could only end in bitter and fruitless fights.

When World War I broke out, word reached remote Kureika that German Socialists had announced support of the Kaiser. Stalin was shocked at this betrayal of international working-class solidarity for raw nationalism. The English and French Socialists also supported their side of the war, and the Second International collapsed. Stalin saw the war simply as a camouflaged imperialistic struggle for markets, colonies, and profits. He hoped for a military defeat of Tsarist Russia, knowing it would speed the day of Revolution.

Russian losses on the Western front were soon so terrible that the desperate Tsarist Army began calling up Siberian exiles. Stalin was not unhappy at being rejected as physically unfit because of a defective left arm. By 1917, the army had suffered almost six million casualties, half of them deaths. In February, the Russian people reached the limit of their endurance. Furious over inflation and starvation wages, sickened by the slaughter of sons and brothers, shocked by scandals at court, goaded by over a million Army deserters and mutineers, the workers of Petersburg once more organized themselves into a Soviet. This time they were supported not only by Russian soldiers but also by the Duma, which hastily set up a new provisional government headed by Alexander Kerensky. The provinces quickly followed the lead of the capital, and a stunned Tsar Nicholas was forced to abdicate.

This bloodless revolution dismayed England and France, who correctly interpreted it to mean the withdrawal of their Russian ally from the war. But from an America still at peace came the pleased voice of President Woodrow Wilson, who spoke of "the wonderful and heartening things that have been happening in the last few weeks in Russia." Wilson saw in the overthrow of the Tsar an echo of the revolt of the thirteen American Colonies against a tyrannical King George. The United States quickly recognized the Kerensky Government, and offered a credit of 325 million dollars.

One of Kerensky's first acts was to release all the political prisoners in Siberia. On March 12th, Stalin arrived back in Petersburg (now called Petrograd) with Kamenev. Lenin was still in exile, in Switzerland; Trotsky had gone to America. Waiting for Lenin's return, Stalin enjoyed the strange sensation of being a revolutionist now free to operate openly.

"You know," he sighed to Kamenev, "one almost misses the Okhrana. Things were a lot more exciting in those days!"

4

Red Star Over Moscow

But there were plenty of fireworks still to come in that stormy year of 1917. Kerensky, a cautious Menshevik, turned a deaf ear to the demand by workers of the Petrograd Soviet for a share of power. He saw the new Russia as a Socialist democracy, not a "dictatorship of the proletariat." The Bolsheviks were angry, but the February Revolution had caught them by surprise. Their leaders were scattered in exile, and most of their rank and file had been drafted into the army.

Stalin found himself almost unknown to the workers of the Petrograd Soviet, many of them illiterate peasants in plaited fiber shoes and coarse handwoven coats. They had been brought from the farms to replace factory workers who had gone to the front. Now they patrolled the streets of the capital, rifles slung on shoulders in ominous warning to the Provisional Government. Stalin also found the Bolshevik Party in Petrograd being run by a group of revolutionary amateurs. He and other veteran Bolshevik leaders returned from exile easily took over the reins of the Party apparatus and reorganized it.

Stalin became editor of *Pravda,* replacing Vyacheslav Molotov, a college student later to become his foreign minister. Kamenev urged that they reverse the Petrograd Soviet's demand that Russia withdraw from the war, cooperating with Kerensky instead. If the war front were allowed to collapse, wouldn't the

Germans simply sweep through Russia and occupy it? What good would the Revolution be then?

Stalin let himself be persuaded by Kamenev's eloquence, and *Pravda* came out in cautious support of Kerensky. A roar of indignation rose from the workers' suburb of Petrograd, and demands were heard for the expulsion of Stalin and Kamenev.

Stalin became deeply worried that he might be making a bad tactical mistake. Each day he warily shifted *Pravda's* position an imperceptible step at a time back to dead centre, ready to jump to whichever side might emerge victorious.

On April 16th, huge searchlights illuminated thousands of soldiers, sailors, and workers as they marched with fluttering Red banners to the Petrograd railway station, welcoming home Russia's most distinguished exile, Nikolai Lenin. He arrived from Germany with his wife, Krupskaya, and other followers in a sealed train. "If the German capitalists are so stupid as to take us over to Russia," Lenin had shrugged, "it's their funeral." The German government had paid him ten million dollars to further the Russian Revolution, hoping in this way to get Russia out of the war so that they would no longer have to fight on two fronts. They counted on Lenin's return to Petrograd to hasten Russia's suit for peace. They were not disappointed.

The huge crowd meeting Lenin's train roared their enthusiasm and sang the "Marseillaise," freedom song of the French Revolution, as Lenin was hoisted onto an armoured car in the glare of a searchlight. He stunned his listeners with a fiery denunciation of *Pravda* and the Petrograd Soviet for not having defied Kerensky; for not calling a strike against the war; for failing to urge seizure of estates, factories, and banks; for playing into the hands of the bourgeoisie by permitting rule by parliamentary republic instead of a workers' Soviet. He urged an immediate fight to the bitter end with Kerensky.

Stalin was stunned. Lenin's homecoming speech had been a humiliating slap in his face as a "foolish Old Bolshevik." Kamenev was indignant, arguing that their master's long exile abroad had caused him to lose touch with Russian realities. Would the Party follow Lenin or the Petrograd leaders? A national Bolshevik Conference, scheduled in eight days, would decide. Meanwhile, Stalin simply gritted his teeth and kept silent, while Kamenev brashly challenged Lenin's views in *Pravda*.

When the conference opened, Lenin's hard brilliance cut his opponents' arguments like a diamond, and it quickly grew evident that his views would prevail in the Party. Now Stalin made his move. Speaking briefly to clarify his position, he criticized Kamenev and urged support for Lenin. This shameless act of opportunism shocked Kamenev, but in Stalin's eyes it was simply a question of political strategy.

The conference elected a new Bolshevik Central Committee of nine members, nucleus of what later became the Politburo, inner cabinet of the Bolshevik Party. Lenin was chosen as its head, along with Grigori Zinoviev, an eloquent Marxist intellectual who had been Lenin's close friend and aide during the long years in exile. The thirty-eight-year-old Stalin, now restored to Lenin's good graces, was also elected. So was Kamenev, who still had strong support. Lenin at once put the committee on record as condemning the policies of the Kerensky government.

On May 17th, cheering crowds turned out at the railroad station again to welcome home another celebrated exile—Leon Trotsky, returning from America. Trotsky delighted Lenin by promptly making a speech to the Petrograd Soviet supporting Lenin's policies. Stalin had still not forgiven Trotsky for snubbing him at Vienna; nevertheless, he proposed that Trotsky be admitted to the Politburo, and this was done. Maybe *that* gesture would melt some of Trotsky's disdain toward him!

But in Trotsky's eyes, Stalin was still a coarse, vulgar peasant whom he contemptuously described as the Party's most accomplished bandit. He continued to ignore Stalin, an example followed by other intellectuals around Lenin. These were highly educated, literate, eloquent men who spoke several languages; the stammering Georgian spoke only Russian in a Caucasian accent that made them wince. Mostly sons of the upper social classes, they were members of an international Socialist elite equally at home in Germany, Austria and Poland. The taciturn provincial, lonely in their midst, developed a fear of their sophisticated European world.

Behind a bland mask that lulled them into viewing him as a dull, plodding party hack, he seethed with envy and resentment. Sensitive to every slight, he patiently hoarded grudges in secret for years until his chance came for retaliation.

"There's nothing sweeter," he once said, "than to bide the proper moment for revenge, insert the knife, twist it, and then go home for a good night's sleep." Painful emotions of inferiority led to much of the brooding, inscrutable behaviour that later baffled the world. This was why he so often spent more energy in destroying fellow Communists than in fighting the international enemies of Soviet Russia. Stalin never forgave any intellectual, except Lenin, his bourgeois background just because he had embraced Communism. What could those born with a silver spoon have in common with those born without *any* spoon?

His humiliation by the Party's well-born intellectuals led him to subscribe sourly to Karl Marx's wry observation, "The rich will do anything for the poor but get off their backs!"

The Bolsheviks worked hard at fanning the discontent of the Russian masses during May and June of 1917. Huge signs were painted on buildings: "Down with the Ten Capitalist Ministers!" and "All Power to the Soviets!" Huge demonstrations demanded Russia's withdrawal from the war. But an American goodwill mission, headed by Elihu Root, told Kerensky bluntly, "No fight, no loan!" In desperation Kerensky ordered Russian troops on the German front to take the offensive. They were hurled back in disastrous defeat, the army in shambles.

Kerensky blamed Lenin. Accusing him and Zinoviev of being German agents, Kerensky ordered their arrest and declared the Bolsheviks illegal. Armed Menshevik groups wrecked Bolshevik headquarters and the offices of *Pravda*. Furious sailors off the *Kronstadt,* quartered at the powerful Peter and Paul Fortress, phoned Stalin to ask whether they should grab their rifles and start an uprising.

"We would only play into Kerensky's hands if we rise before Lenin gives the signal," Stalin calmed them. "Keep cool and don't worry. I won't let them arrest Lenin!"

The Menshevik forces sought Lenin everywhere, but he was concealed in the apartment of Stalin's old friend Alliluyev while Stalin aranged an escape to Finland. To make certain Lenin would not be recognized aboard the train, Stalin turned barber and shaved off the fugitive's beard and moustache. As Lenin left, he told Stalin that he would relay orders for the Central Committee through him. For a while, Stalin himself was practically the whole Politburo, because Trotsky, Kamenev and most of the other Bolshevik leaders had been caught and imprisoned. Only Stalin was wily enough to escape by keeping himself in the background of Party activity—a "gray blur," Trotsky designated him contemptuously.

By the end of July, however, persecution of Bolshevik leaders had won the Party such support that Stalin was able to call a semisecret Congress attended by delegates representing 240,000 members. They debated whether to seize power at once or wait until Europe's Socialists revolted and ended the war. "We ought to discard the obsolete idea that only Europe can show us the way," Stalin argued. "Why should not Russia give the example to the world?" He won the vote of the Congress, but the question of whether Socialism could be built first in Russia was to continue agitating Bolshevik leaders, who quarrelled over It for the next quarter of a century.

Lenin believed with Trotsky that the downfall of world capitalism was inevitable. But Lenin also felt that each country had to develop its own timetable for revolution, because, he argued, revolution cannot be exported. Trotsky, however, claimed that the Russian Bolsheviks had to give priority to world revolution because a Socialist Russia standing alone would be destroyed by capitalist encirclement. Stalin was convinced that the chief task of the Party was to build a powerful Soviet Russia—and devil take the rest of the world!

Lenin sent his messages from Finland to the apartment of Alliluyev. Stalin moved in with his old friend so that he could receive, answer, and act upon these notes swiftly. He gradually became aware of Alliluyev's daughter Nadya, now no longer a child but an attractive young adolescent of sixteen. Despite the twenty-two years' difference in their ages, the widowed Georgian found himself smitten by Nadya's charms, and began to dream of marrying again. Nadya, in turn, was awed by her father's old comrade, about whom she had heard so many tales.

But as always with Russia's man of steel, the Revolution came first. Bolshevik prestige was soaring. Trotsky, released from prison, was elected President of the Petrograd Soviet, the same position he had held in the 1905 Revolution. In Finland, Lenin became convinced that revolution was imminent in Germany and Italy, and began to bombard Stalin with messages urging an immediate Bolshevik uprising in Petrograd. "It is for us to begin," he exhorted in mid-September. "Delay becomes positively a crime!"

But the Politburo hesitated, made anxious by the insistence of Kamenev and Zinoviev that if the Bolsheviks seized power now, they would not be able to hold on to it. The timidity of his followers made Lenin furious. Determined to force them to act, he returned secretly to Petrograd, disguised by make-up, a wig and glasses. "If 130,000 landowners were able to govern Russia in the interests of the rich," he lashed out at his colleagues sarcastically, "then certainly 240,000 Bolsheviks can govern it for the benefit of the poor!"

Stalin quickly sensed that Lenin's magnetic personality was again going to carry the day. He voted with ten of the twelve Party members present for an immediate armed uprising. Zinoviev and Kamenev voted against Lenin, and were so incensed at the Politburo's decision that they resigned and even exposed the secret by attacking it openly in a newspaper article.

Lenin denounced them bitterly as traitors and strikebreakers. Disturbed and worried by this split, Stalin tried to heal the breach with a conciliatory editorial in *Pravda,* but only incurred Lenin's wrath for his "weakness." On October 24th, government troops suddenly took over the offices of *Pravda* and silenced its presses. Kerensky issued orders for the arrest of all Politburo leaders, who had now become members of a new Military Revolutionary Committee. But Kerensky had inexplicably moved too late, despite the public warning by Zinoviev and Kamenev. By now the Bolsheviks had won over most of Petrograd's soldiers, sailors and workers.

The famous October Revolution erupted at 2:00 a.m. on October 25, 1917. These "ten days that shook the world"—in the words of John Reed, a young American reporter and sympathizer—actually began on November 7th, but the Julian calendar then in use in Russia was dated two weeks earlier.

Storm centre of the Revolution was the Smolny Institute, a girls' school on the banks of the river, some distance from the centre of Petrograd. Here Bolshevik excitement rose to fever pitch in response to fiery speeches delivered around the clock to a new All-Russian Bolshevik Congress. Regiments of Red Guards—soldiers, sailors, and workmen with rifles—were ordered to seize the capital's strategic strong points one at a time. The Red troops met no opposition as they swarmed over the telegraph agency, state bank, post office, power stations and bridges. The Smolny Congress greeted reports of each new victory with giant roars and cheers.

Now Lenin came out into the open, fugitive no longer, master of the capital of Russia. He proclaimed the slogan of the

Revolution *"All power to the Soviets!"* From the Winter Palace, a frightened Kerensky slipped out of the city in an American Embassy car draped with an American flag, hoping to rally troops outside Petrograd to march in against the Bolsheviks.

The cruiser *Aurora,* which had gone over to the Revolution, began lobbing shells at the Winter Palace from the Neva. Then Red Guards stormed inside, quickly forcing the Kerensky cabinet to resign at gunpoint. John Reed, who had dashed into the Palace with the troops, saw them smashing open bureau drawers with the butts of their guns, and dragging off fine carpets, linen and china. An outraged Party member shouted, "Comrades, keep your hands off! That is now the property of the people!" But special armed guards with pistols drawn, at the Palace entrance, had to search and strip the looters of all their booty.

Although the Revolution was accomplished with little bloodshed, the shellfire, the confusion of twenty thousand armed Red Guards running through the streets, the desertion of garrisons, and the exchange of rifle fire, all left no doubt that a civil war had taken place. "The Bolsheviks got the city in their hands," an anguished butler of the American Ambassador wrote home, "and I want to tell you it is something awful!"

In twenty-four hours, the Bolsheviks were in complete command of the capital of Russia, and word reached Stalin that Bolshevik uprisings were going on in many other cities as well. When Lenin rose to speak to the Smolny Congress, he was greeted with a prolonged, enthusiastic roar.

Then, in a quiet voice that echoed around the world, he said, "We shall now proceed to construct the Socialist order."

Lenin issued a Decree of Peace on behalf of the new "Workers' and Peasants' Government," calling on all nations for an immediate armistice to negotiate an end to the World War. This clearly hinted at Russia's withdrawal from the war. Lenin observed that the Russian Army had already voted against war with their feet, referring to the great number of deserters back from the front.

Uprisings swept through one city after another, and anarchy and bloodshed became the order of the day. As in the French Revolution, the worst elements of the masses—including thieves and murderers—smashed into homes, stores and buildings. Pretending to represent the new government, they killed all who resisted and looted everything in sight. No decently dressed Russian was safe from attack on the streets. When some Politburo members grew indignant, Stalin shrugged and reminded them of Lenin's favourite axiom, "You can't make an omelet without breaking eggs." But the revolutionary chaos drove thousands of technicians, managers, and professionals to flight. Factories stopped running, and hunger spread as peasants refused to part with food to feed the idle cities.

Stalin had played only a minor part in the actual Revolution, with the starring roles in the hands of Lenin and Trotsky. Through most of it Stalin sat outside the door of Lenin's office like a sentry, keeping a careful eye on everyone who entered and left. But Lenin had a special job in mind for him in the new Council of People's Commissars. Lenin had made himself Chairman, or Prime Minister; Trotsky had the Foreign Affairs portfolio; and Kamenev, as a gesture of Party unity, was made President of the Republic. Lenin made Stalin the Commissar for Nationalities with a joke to the council: "No intelligence is needed for that, which is why we've put Stalin there." The Georgian pretended to share the council's laughter, but the thrust hurt. He silently vowed to make his Commissariat one of the most important in the council, and he did.

With the Russian throne toppled and bourgeois power swept away with Kerensky, many of Russia's various nationalities now began to insist upon their right to break away as independent nations. They had supported the Bolsheviks, confident that the

Revolution would free them from the Russian yoke. But Lenin knew that a Soviet Russia stripped of its national minorities could never become a great power. He relied increasingly upon Stalin to persuade the fiercely nationalistic Russian provinces to remain in, and to support, a centralized Soviet Government. The loss of Finland was inevitable because it had always been autonomous within the Russian Empire, united to Moscow only by bonds of royalty. Poland, too, would have to be freed because of the intensity of the Poles' anti-Russian feeling. But Lenin counted on Stalin to see to it that the new Soviet regime lost no other territories.

The new Commissar of Nationalities began his control over 65 million of Russia's 140 million people in a room at the Smolny, seated at a bare table around which he soon gathered Georgians, Uzbeks, Ukrainians, and Kazakhs to help him hold the nation's minorities under the Red Star. Stalin was chief architect of the idea of a "Union" of Socialist Soviet Republics (USSR), in which each republic elected its own government and officials, while real power remained in the hands of tough Russian Party bosses appointed from Moscow or Petrograd. Stalin and Lenin were no more prepared to let Russia's provinces secede from this Soviet Union than Lincoln had been willing to let the Southern states secede from the United States.

The coming to power of the Bolsheviks, and the moves toward peace, infuriated some generals and other Right Wing elements who threatened a counterrevolution. Lenin moved swiftly to crush them, with Stalin constantly at his side as his aide, observing, studying, imitating. "At Tiflis I was a school-boy," Stalin admitted later. "At Baku I turned into an apprentice. But in Petrograd under Lenin I became a craftsman!" So closely did he identify with his idol that when he finally won power he circulated the slogan: "Stalin Is Lenin Today!"

At Lenin's feet in 1917, he also learned how to purge political enemies. Lenin created a secret police bureau called the Cheka, headed by Felix Dzerzhinsky, a fierce Polish Social Democrat. Once at a Party meeting, Lenin passed Stalin a note for Dzerzhinsky asking how many "reactionaries" were being held in Moscow's jails. The Cheka chief wrote the number fifteen hundred and handed it to Stalin, who gave it back to Lenin. Observing Lenin mark the note with a cross, Dzerzhinsky jumped up, left the hall and ordered the instant execution of fifteen hundred prisoners.

When Stalin discovered this, he asked Dzerzhinsky incredulously, "Didn't you know that Lenin marks all communications with a cross simply to show that he's understood them?"

Dzerzhinsky blinked, then smiled. "Oh, well, it doesn't really matter. Now Lenin has fifteen hundred enemies less to worry about."

Joseph Stalin learned from Dzerzhinsky, too.

5

Americans in Siberia

For six hours every day, Stalin joined other Red leaders in turning the new Russia upside down with a flood of new laws pouring out of Smolny. Banks and factories were nationalized; government debts were repudiated; wages were fixed; courts were replaced by revolutionary tribunals; church marriages were replaced by civil ceremonies; church lands were confiscated. All titles were abolished, and by law everyone was now to be addressed as "Citizen" or "Comrade."

Neither Lenin, Trotsky nor Stalin had any real notion of how to enforce these laws, or what would happen if they did. "We'll just learn from experience," Lenin blithely suggested.

But the Russian people, excited by their first free elections in November, shocked the Bolsheviks by giving them only a fourth of the vote. Half the members elected to the new Constituent Assembly were Social Revolutionaries, who had promised rule by a democratic parliament. Stalin grumbled to Lenin that their revolution was being taken away from them. Had they overthrown Kerensky simply to remain a powerless minority party? When the new parliament met at Petrograd's Tauride Palace in January, 1918, Bolshevik troops suddenly seized the palace, turned the lights out and dissolved the Assembly. Lenin, Trotsky, and Stalin then ruled Russia as an "Executive Committee."

Lenin named Trotsky as Foreign Minister and sent him to Brest-Litovsk to conclude a peace treaty with the Germans. Trotsky made the mistake of haggling over terms, hoping that delay would bring a German Army revolt against the Kaiser. Stalin warned Lenin that Trotsky was playing a dangerous game. He was right. Snubbing Trotsky, the Germans thrust through the defenceless Russian lines, occupying Estonia, parts of Latvia, Poland, Romania, and the Ukraine. Their terms for peace stiffened as they speared closer to Petrograd. Trotsky frantically wired Lenin for instructions. But now Lenin made Trotsky wait until he consulted Stalin, on whose advice the Russians finally paid Germany's price to let them out of the war. The humiliating Brest-Litovsk treaty forced Russia to yield a quarter of her territory containing a third of her population and croplands, a quarter of her resources, over half her industries.

From then on Stalin and Trotsky feuded bitterly, each vying for the role of chief lieutenant to Lenin. Stalin's star rose steadily because he was the more cunning plotter. Cautious about getting out on a limb, he was also adroit at retreating to safe positions, diverting any blame to a scapegoat. Trotsky was more of a bull in a china shop, blustering into pitfalls with rash courage, then screaming in rage at the narrow-eyed Georgian "brigand of the Caucasus" he hated and despised. Because Lenin needed them both, he soothed first one, then the other.

The new Red government moved to Moscow in March, 1918. Wandering through the great spaces of the Kremlin in his rough peasant blouse and boots, Stalin could not help musing on his fantastic climb from a village hovel in Gori to this fairyland of richly carved beds, halls decorated in gleaming gold, ivory thrones and sceptres and crowns encrusted with diamonds. A single man, the Tsar, had once been supreme ruler of this mighty seat of empire. Could not another Russian, shrewd and patient enough, also make it all his own?

Dissatisfied with the small office allotted to him in the Kremlin, Stalin told Nadya Alliluyev, who now worked in his Commissariat, to type out a dozen notices reading: "these quarters occupied by the PEOPLE'S commissariat of nationalities." With an assistant named Pestkovsky, he rode at midnight to the Great Siberian Hotel, which had been taken over by another Soviet ministry. Ripping off a paper sign on the door, he tacked on one of his own. Then they broke into the rear of the hotel. Pestkovsky lit their way with matches as Stalin tacked more notices on doors and columns until they ran out of matches and Stalin almost fell down a staircase in the dark. The next day, he moved his staff into their new requisitioned quarters.

The nation was seething with turmoil and discontent over the German occupation, famine, worthless money, unemployment, the refusal of peasants to send food to the cities. Soviet leaders in the Ukraine, Cossack country, and Transcaucasus were mostly Mensheviks or Social Revolutionaries, who ignored or defied Bolshevik edicts from Moscow. To enforce these edicts, Lenin had to send out Party officials armed with dictatorial powers. But these plenipotentiaries could not stop civil war.

Red armies in the south of Russia were challenged by White armies led by Bolshevik-hating generals secretly backed by England and France, who hoped to overthrow the Lenin regime and bring Russia back into the war against Germany. The West also hoped, in the words of France's Premier Clémenceau, to protect Europe from the germs of Bolshevism in the East. Lenin sent Trotsky into the field as Commander-in-Chief of the Red Army, keeping Stalin by his side in the Kremlin to utilize the Georgian's genius for Party organization and planning. But Stalin fretted at being so far from the excitement of battle, deskbound while his archrival Trotsky cut a colourful figure in the field as a military hero. At heart Stalin was still Koba, the revolutionary outlaw who delighted in danger as he raced two steps ahead of the Okhrana.

Wearied by all the talk that buzzed around him in the Kremlin, Stalin often excused himself from Party meetings "for just one moment." He would vanish for the day to some friend's kitchen, where he would lie on a divan, smoking his pipe moodily. His chance to escape from Moscow came at last in April. The food supply for Moscow and Petrograd, shipped up the Volga from southern Russia, was suddenly threatened by White armies converging on Tsaritsyn (later Stalingrad.)

Lenin rushed Stalin to Tsaritsyn to mobilize the collection of wheat surpluses and speed it northward. If the White Russians took the city, they would be able to starve the Red regime out of power. Arriving in Tsaritsyn with two armoured trains and a detachment of Red Guards, Stalin found the city in wild disorder. He telegraphed Lenin: I AM BULLYING AND SWEARING AT ALL THOSE WHO NEED IT . . . WHATEVER HAPPENS WE WILL SEND YOU WHEAT. IF OUR MILITARY SPECIALISTS (WHO ARE BLOCKHEADS) HAD NOT BEEN IDLE OR ASLEEP, OUR LINE WOULD NEVER HAVE BEEN PIERCED. This spiteful thrust at Trotsky was not without some justification. Lacking experienced commanders for the Red Army, Trotsky had recruited thirty thousand officers of the old Imperial Army. Not surprisingly, many sabotaged resistance against White Russian troops instead of fighting them.

Visiting the four-hundred-mile front, Stalin became convinced that Tsaritsyn could not be held without a drastic military shakeup. He also shrewdly recognized an opportunity to inflate his own military prestige at Trotsky's expense. Writing to Lenin on June 10th, he warned that because of Trotsky's blunder "within a month everything in the North Caucasus will crash and this region will be lost to us indefinitely. . . . I need full military authority. I have already written about this but received no reply. Very good. I myself will, without formalities, dismiss those commanders who are ruining the situation. . . . The absence of a piece of paper from Trotsky will not stop me!"

Stalin's first step in this bold power play was to use the Cheka to arrest Party officials and Red Army commanders he did not trust. He ordered tighter discipline among all troops, and personally reorganized all plans of defence and counterattack. Unlike Trotsky, he never personally made rousing speeches to troops, but operated behind the scenes, exerting pressure by secret manipulations. Sleeping rarely, he divided his time between Army Headquarters and the battlefronts.

Once when his authority was challenged he growled, "Here it is, who am Lenin!" He made lightning judgments of men, promoting Party agitators abruptly to commissars and officials. The reorganized defenders of Tsaritsyn began to fight spiritedly, possibly because Stalin cut off further retreat by sending all available barges loaded with grain to Moscow. He and his men were left with two possibilities—victory or starvation. The White Russian attackers were stopped and hurled back beyond the Don River. A delighted Lenin appointed Stalin military commander of the Tsaritsyn front. Trotsky fired an angry telegram to Lenin through Tsaritsyn headquarters. Stalin coolly wrote across it, "To be disregarded."

The Ural Russians had never forgotten that Tsar Nicholas had once ordered his armies to kill several thousand men, women and children of Siberia and the Urals as revenge for the 1905 Revolution. On July 16th, armed peasants and workers of the Ekaterinburg Soviet dragged the Royal Family out of a jail in the Urals and put them before a firing squad. Lenin shrugged.

Two weeks later, as though in outraged response to the murder of the Romanovs, the British and French intervened openly in the Russian civil war. From Finnish Murmansk, they invaded Archangel on the White Sea, using the port as a base for White Russian operations. In response to Anglo-French pressures, American troops also arrived.

President Wilson was told they were needed to protect Allied war supplies in Murmansk from falling into German hands, and to block Japan from seizing parts of Siberia. But the British and French commands cynically used the seven thousand American troops as anti-Bolshevik forces. The American expedition remained in northern Russia for a year and a half, bewildered as to why they were there and who was the enemy.

Lenin was understandably furious at the West's intervention in Russia's civil war. He raged publicly against "the beasts of prey of Anglo-French and American imperialism" for "prolonging the imperialist slaughter" of the World War. *Pravda* accused the United States of interfering in the Revolution because of the interests of the New York Stock Exchange.

Stalin, meanwhile, continued to direct military operations on the Tsaritsyn front, where he found himself among old Georgian friends from his days as a Bolshevik agitator on the Baku oil fields. Chief among them were Kliment Voroshilov, commander of the Tenth Army, and Semeon Budenny, a cavalry commander. The rough, tough "Tsaritsyn group" insolently ignored directives from Trotsky's headquarters in Kozlov. Outraged, Trotsky threatened them with dire punishment. He telegraphed Lenin:

I INSIST CATEGORICALLY ON STALIN'S RECALL. THINGS ARE GOING BADLY ON THE TSARITSYN FRONT . . . NO SERIOUS ACTION WILL BE POSSIBLE WITHOUT COORDINATION FROM TSARITSYN . . . THERE IS UTTER ANARCHY AT THE TOP.

Lenin could not tolerate the feud between his two chief lieutenants much longer. Since Trotsky was Supreme Commander in the field, it was he who would have to be supported. But to sweeten the pill, Lenin waited until mid-October, when the danger to Tsaritsyn was past. Then he sent President of the Republic Jacob Sverdlov to bring Stalin back to Moscow in a special train decorated in honor of the hero of Tsaritsyn.

To try to reconcile the two rivals, Sverdlov managed to have Trotsky's train and Stalin's train cross paths, and he arranged a meeting in Trotsky's private car. Stalin was meek and conciliatory, but Trotsky snapped coldly that he intended to fire Voroshilov and Budenny. Stalin swallowed his fury behind the placid mask he wore to keep his feelings hidden.

"Do you really want to dismiss both of them?" he asked mildly. "They're fine boys."

"Those fine boys of yours," Trotsky flared, "will ruin the Revolution, which can't wait for them to grow up!"

When Germany finally surrendered to the Allies in November, 1918, the Soviet Government lost no time in annulling the Brest-Litovsk treaty. Lenin demanded the evacuation of Soviet territory overrun by the Germans. Woodrow Wilson supported this demand over the objections of Winston Churchill, now British Secretary of War, who ordered Allied squadrons to enter the Black Sea. Churchill's hopes for overthrowing the Soviet Union rested with two White Russian commanders—Anton Denikin, self-proclaimed "dictator of Russia," and Admiral A. V. Kolchak. Churchill blocked the seating of the Soviets at the Versailles Peace Conference, refused to recognize Lenin's regime, and sought to surround Russia with hostile governments.

When French troops landed in Odessa on December 17th, Maxim Litvinov of the Soviet foreign office appealed to President Wilson to use his influence to stop foreign intervention in Russia. Kolchak's White forces, meanwhile, were threatening the whole eastern front. Lenin rushed Stalin, accompanied by Cheka head Felix Dzerzhinsky, to save the situation. Stalin found the Third Red Army a defeated ruin, many of its officers drunk and openly cooperating with the enemy. He promptly set up firing squads for hundreds of suspected renegades. After that he never trusted any Red Army unit without a watchful political commissar reporting secretly to Moscow.

By January, 1919, Stalin had whipped the Third Army back into fighting shape, checked Kolchak's advance, and started a successful counteroffensive. But once again he infuriated Trotsky by ignoring the Red Army Commander-in-Chief's directives; Trotsky bitterly insisted upon his recall. Lenin waited until the Ural front was secure, then "invited" Stalin back to Moscow to report on his successful operation.

Soon after his return, Trotsky's spies gleefully informed him that Stalin was secretly drinking wine from the Tsar's cellars below the Kremlin. The sale of alcoholic beverages in Russia was at that time illegal. Trotsky complained to Lenin, "If the rumour reaches the front that there is drinking in the Kremlin, it will make a bad impression!" Lenin called Stalin to account for his raids on the cellar.

"How do you expect Caucasians to get along without wine?" Stalin shrugged. Lenin smiled and nodded.

Trotsky glumly understood that he had lost again.

In the middle of the civil war, Stalin suddenly made up his mind to marry Nadya Alliluyev, the quiet, modest young daughter of his old friend. Never too comfortable with women, he simply suggested to her that they would make a "well-suited" married couple. Overwhelmed, she consented and became his second wife. They took up quarters in a simple lodging of the Kremlin once occupied by servants of the Tsar.

Nadya retained her maiden name, as the law allowed, wanting no favor or advancement of her own career simply because she was Stalin's wife. Attending a technical college in Moscow, she ate lunch with other students who did not know her identity, received a diploma as a commercial engineer, and won a subordinate administrative post on her own merits. Stalin loved her as much as his steely nature permitted him to feel deep emotion for anyone. They had two children—a daughter called Zveitlana and a son, Vassily. Like most Russian families of important men, Nadya and the children kept out of the public eye, but Moscow knew that the Stalins were a genuinely devoted couple. Patient Nadya was unruffled by Stalin's occasional outbursts of hot temper and Georgian sarcasm.

President Wilson sent a diplomat, William G. Bullitt, on a secret mission to Moscow in mid-March to see what could be done to untangle the Russian problem for the Allies. Bullitt found Lenin cooperative. The two men worked out a plan to end the undeclared war between the West and Russia, raise the Allied blockade of Soviet ports, withdraw all foreign troops, end the civil war, and grant amnesty to all White Russian forces. Bullitt rushed back to Washington jubilantly, only to find Wilson too seriously ill to see him. Wilson's assistant, Colonel House, brusquely turned Bullitt over to the State Department. Anti-Russian officials heard the peace plan in silence, then pigeon-holed it. Shocked and embittered, Bullitt resigned in protest. Fourteen years later he was recalled to government service by President Roosevelt to become the first US ambassador to the Soviet Union.

Disgusted at being let down by Bullitt, Lenin called a world conference of revolutionists in Moscow in the spring of 1919. He set up a Third International, or "Comintern," replacing the old Socialist Second International, which had died with the outbreak of war. Lenin now felt that if Communist Russia was to survive, it would need revolutionary governments in Europe as allies. Even if other Communist regimes did not come to power, a Moscow-controlled Comintern would be a useful weapon in Lenin's hands against the West, weakening them from within. Zinoviev was made President. Later that year, the Comintern created an American Communist Party, Lenin and Zinoviev hailing it as a great step forward for the world.

The civil war continued to rage through the spring and summer of 1919, French troops joining the White Russians in fierce attacks on the Red Army. Kolchak and Denikin scored sweeping victories. Russian villagers hearing an army approach would drive off their cattle to a hiding place while scouts were sent out to learn if the troops were Red or White. Red troops would be welcomed by a "village Soviet," with the priest conspicuously absent. White troops were met by a Council of Elders led by a priest carrying a holy ikon. In either case, the cattle remained prudently hidden until the army had gone.

General N. Yudenich's White Armies, supported by shell-fire from British warships, swept toward Petrograd. The Red Army fell back in panic, and leaders of two forts commanding the city's heights went over to the enemy. Stalin and Trotsky sped to the battlefront. Trotsky promptly ordered every tenth Red Army man shot to stiffen resistance. He made flaming speeches to workers and troops preparing to fight in the streets and squares, warning that if Petrograd's heavy industries were lost, the whole Soviet regime would crumble.

Stalin's firing squads also worked overtime. Tearing up military defence plans shown him by the General Staff, he devised a new strategy to break the siege by a surprise Red Navy attack on the two forts in Yudenich's hands. Military specialists argued against the plan as "an impossibility of naval science." But Stalin's idea worked; the Yudenich attack crumbled and Petrograd was saved. Lenin happily ordered decorations for both Stalin and Trotsky. Proud of having taught the General Staff professionals a lesson, Stalin from then on felt supremely confident in his own military judgment.

He was so sure of himself now that in June, 1919, he finally dared challenge Trotsky openly. He demanded that the Party's Central Committee transfer command of the southern front to him, and warn Trotsky not to interfere with him in any way. The Committee, however, took its cue from Lenin and gave the outraged Trotsky a vote of confidence. Stalin secretly expected this verdict, but he enjoyed being able to defy Trotsky on equal terms. As a sign of Lenin's new respect for Stalin as strategist, the Central Committee accepted a plan he put forth to change Soviet tactics on the southern front. His star rose even higher when this new strategy pushed Denikin's armies into the Black Sea, saving the Ukraine. Now the Red Army began to take the offensive everywhere, and the White Armies of Yudenich and Kolchak rapidly fell apart.

Gloom assailed London and Paris, where it was now apparent that the gamble of Western intervention in Russia had failed, and that the Soviet Government was going to endure. Disgusted at the way the British command in Archangel had used his American troops in Russia, Wilson firmly announced his intention to withdraw them as soon as weather permitted. The Americans had fought only futile skirmishes with Bolshevik forces, and now faced a terrible Arctic winter with temperatures that dropped to fifty below zero. Huddled miserably in snow-smothered blockhouses in the wintry forests, they waited hopefully for spring and home.

Stalin was awarded the Order of the Red Banner for his military brilliance in saving the Soviet Union from its enemies within and without. He never forgot that American troops had invaded Russian soil with Anglo-French forces, and had been used to try to overthrow the Soviet regime.Stalin did not know, nor would he have believed, that Wilson had been duped about the purposes for which American troops were to be used.

Joseph Stalin nursed his distrust of America, a tragedy that poisoned world peace, until his death forty years later.

6

In Lenin's Shadow

Was the end of the civil war, Stalin wondered warily, anything more than a breathing space? The Allied armies were indeed gone . . . but for how long? Could the capitalist powers permit a proletariat revolution to succeed and survive, offering a dangerous example to their own workers?

The Bolsheviks were caught in a paradox of their own. As much as they feared and suspected the West, they needed the West even more. The civil war had left Russia in ruins. Everything was in such a state of disrepair that the tenements of Moscow and Petrograd were collapsing, and grass was sprouting in the streets. Trotsky wanted to turn the Red Army into a forced labour corps under military discipline.

If the Bolshevik regime was to survive, it would need credits from the major capitalist powers to put the nation back on its feet. This meant at least a temporary policy of coexistence with the West. But Trotsky felt that Russia should be promoting Western revolution, not Western loans. Lenin argued that they could get the credits, aid, and trade they needed just by playing off the capitalist governments against each other. Stalin agreed that the lust for profit would prevent a united front against Moscow. The foreign intervention had fallen apart he felt, because each Western nation was secretly more interested in getting an inside track on Russian trade. Besides, Stalin asked slyly, was there any reason they couldn't deal with the capitalist governments in the market place, while secretly helping Communist Parties of the West?

In the West, meanwhile, statesmen who had opposed military intervention in Russia were now being listened to more respectfully. "We have failed to restore Russia to sanity by force," Lloyd George told the British parliament in February, 1920. "I believe we can save her by trade. Commerce has a sobering influence. . . . Trade, in my opinion, will bring an end to the ferocity, the rapine, and the crudity of Bolshevism surer than any other method."

On the day before an Anglo-Soviet trade agreement was signed in March, 1921, Kamenev cynically told the Tenth Party Congress in Moscow, "We are convinced that the foreign capitalists will be obliged to work on the terms we offer them. . . . Foreign capital will fulfill the role Marx predicted for it. . . . With every additional shovel of coal, with every additional load of oil that we in Russia obtain through the help of foreign technique, capital will be digging its own grave."

There was a curious postscript to the civil war and foreign intervention. The Versailles Treaty had created a new independent Polish nation out of lands which for a century had been divided among Prussia, Austria and Russia. Poland's border with Russia, later known as the Curzon Line, was in question because Russia, uninvited to the Peace Conference, had not been there to ratify it. The Poles, led by Marshal Jozef Pilsudski, had stayed out of the Russian civil war, content with the spectacle of an increasingly weakened Russian bear. But when the Bolshevik regime finally staggered to victory, Pilsudski suddenly decided to attack. He reasoned that the Reds would be in no position to resist a surprise thrust, and Poland would now be able to push its eastern border far into Russian territory. News of the attack in April, 1920, stunned the Western powers, who were exasperated at Pilsudski for undertaking such a mad adventure, expecting to succeed where the mighty West had failed.

At first the Polish invasion caught the Russians so flat-footed that by May 7th, Kiev was captured. Stalin was rushed to the southern front to save the situation. By June, his forces had recaptured Kiev, and the unhappy Poles were in full retreat toward Warsaw, hotly pursued by the Red Army. Trotsky favoured ending the war on this triumphant note, and for once Stalin agreed. "I regard the bragging and harmful complacency which some comrades are guilty of as unwarranted," he told the Politburo. "Some of them are not satisfied with the successes at the front but shout about 'a march on Warsaw' This simply doesn't fit the military possibilities or the policy of the Soviet Government."

But Lenin wanted to "probe Europe with the bayonets of the Red Army," hoping to throw a Communist bridge across Poland that would encourage the Communists in defeated Germany to seize power. Hearing this, Stalin quickly changed his mind. So the Red Army plunged on into Poland, and Pilsudski appealed frantically to the West for help. The disgusted Allies felt that Poland's plight served her right, but grudgingly sent munitions and military advisers. The Red Army suffered a shattering defeat in a battle on the Vistula, and reeled back out of Poland. The two sides, weary and disillusioned, finally signed an armistice in October, agreeing on a mutual frontier. Stalin bitterly blamed Trotsky and his General Staff for the Vistula fiasco, while Trotsky accused Stalin of ignoring directives . . . "as usual!" Neither dared blame Lenin for wanting the Polish invasion in the first place.

Stalin returned wearily to a Moscow, now so excoriated that the water mains had burst, caving holes in the streets and depriving the city of running water and steam heat. He found people burning their own furniture, doors and flooring to keep from freezing to death in the thirty-below winter. Wherever he looked, he saw men, women and children in tatters, on the verge of starvation. There was little to eat but cheap dried fish and mouldy bread; a great famine was sweeping across the rich agricultural regions. The peasants were hoarding food and refusing to send it to the cities. At the same time that a million Russian workers were deserting shutdown factories to return to rural villages, millions of peasants were swarming away from the farms all along the Volga, driven by hunger and pestilence.

In March, 1921, the sailors of the Kronstadt naval base, on the outskirts of Petrograd, grew weary of the famine rations allowed them under "War Communism" regulations, and mutinied. Sons of poor peasants, they were the same sailors who had helped the Bolsheviks seize power in the October Revolution, now deeply disillusioned by the plight of the peasantry under the Red Star. They were quelled after fierce attacks by Red Army forces, but the impact of their unexpected revolt shook the new rulers in the Kremlin. Stalin knew then that the Bolsheviks had reached the limits of Russian tolerance, and would now have to act swiftly to pacify the people.

At that time, Herbert Hoover was heading the American Relief Administration, which had undertaken to distribute food to a large part of hungry postwar Europe. Maxim Litvinov was ordered to appeal for help to Washington. Hoover, who had small love for the Communists, nevertheless saw Litvinov's request as an opportunity to bargain for a Soviet pledge to stop agitating outside its borders and to stop punishing White Russians. Litvinov bitterly accused Hoover of using food as a weapon to weaken the Soviet Government.

Despite distrust on both sides, a treaty was signed, and up to ten million Russian men, women and children were kept from starving by American food distributed with the help of a hundred thousand Russians employed by Hoover's ARA. Afterward, Stalin ordered the arrest of hundreds of these workers as spies and counterrevolutionaries for America. Some may well have been, but Stalin's real motive was to discredit America's humanitarian image in Russian eyes. Hoover was so outraged by the

Kremlin's churlish ingratitude that he peevishly refused to recognize the Soviet Union when he became President.

Stalin's sharp eye was fixed on another threat to Bolshevik hegemony—his own native Georgia. Unlike most of Russia, the Georgian province had resisted sovietization, and was still being ruled by Mensheviks, although their power was waning. Stalin suddenly ordered the Second Red Army to invade Georgia and put the Menshevik leaders to flight. Then he went to Tiflis himself to exhort his fellow Georgians against "Menshevik treason." The Georgians were sullen and resentful, bitter at having been invaded by Russian troops sent against them by one of their own kind. They booed and jeered him, and many sprang to the platform to denounce him as a traitor to Georgian independence. Shocked, Stalin fell grimly silent when even his old school chum Iremashvili flung angry accusations at him as the crowd roared approval. Never before or afterward did he endure such public condemnation and humiliation.

"All of Georgia must be ploughed under!" he snarled at Dzerzhinsky. The Cheka began to purge not only Tiflis Mensheviks but also Bolsheviks "infected by local nationalism." Using the authority of the Politburo, Stalin elevated to power in Georgia a group of his oldest and most trusted cronies. Only much later did Lenin discover with a sense of shock that many of his own most devoted supporters had been purged, replaced by Stalin men. With infinite cunning and patience, the wily Georgian was spinning the first strands of the fine web in which he hoped one day to trap the greatest Soviet prize.

Returning to Moscow, he was more than a little stunned to hear Lenin tell the Politburo that, in order to get Russia moving out of its postwar chaos and stagnation, they would have to halt sovietization and restore private enterprise for peasants and Russian capitalists. "It is only a temporary retreat," Lenin explained. "We have to take one step backward in order to take two steps forward. The cities and towns are starving and the peasants refuse to produce more food than they need. For the time being they have beaten us. We have no choice but retreat. One day we shall resume the advance."

Veteran Bolshevik leaders protested angrily that this was tantamount to betraying the Revolution. Stalin quickly recovered from his own astonishment and seconded Lenin vigorously, less because he believed Lenin right than because Lenin's gratitude was important to his secret ambitions.

The New Economic Policy, or NEP, introduced a whole new look to the Soviet economy, one which startled the world as much as the Russian people themselves. Private trade and small-scale private industry, driven by the carrot of personal profit, began to turn the wheels of the Russian economy. No longer compelled to deliver surplus food to requisitioning gangs from the cities, peasants were now able to trade it for manufactured goods. Hoarded capital came out of hiding to open shops, factories, bakeries and restaurants. The new capitalism under Communism began to change the face of Russia.

"If we had not transformed our economic policy," Lenin admitted to the Eleventh Party Congress, "we should not have lasted many months longer." Lenin also sought a truce with the Russian Orthodox Church by stopping any further confiscation of its ancient treasures. In gratitude, Patriarch Tikhon recognized the Bolshevik regime and ordered priests to include the Government in their prayers, as they had done for the Tsar.

Although the NEP brought a great economic surge forward to a nation paralyzed by world war, revolution and foreign invasion, it also gave rise to all kinds of graft, rackets and violations of regulations. Trotsky demanded a sharp crackdown on these practices, with tight controls on all workers,

Stalin sarcastically observed that he was "too flushed with the success of the military method." The proper method of correction, Stalin insisted, was persuasion. Lenin agreed to let him head a new Workers-Peasants Inspection Department, nicknamed Rabkrin. Stalin's idea of persuasion involved the use of undercover agents to spy out and shoot NEP violators until he earned a reprimand from Lenin.

Despite a preoccupation with internal affairs, Stalin did not lose sight of the importance of the Soviet image in world eyes. He strongly supported Lenin's decision to sign the Treaty of Rapallo with Germany and Austria in 1922, indicating to the West that Russia did not feel bound by the Versailles Treaty. It was also a hint that if the West remained reluctant to help the Soviet with credits, their former enemies were not. Foreign correspondent Walter Duranty, in a dispatch to *The New York Times,* accurately interpreted the Rapallo Treaty as a clear sign that the Soviet Union was on the way to becoming a great force in world affairs.

Trotsky kept insisting that the foreign intervention proved that the USSR would never be safe in a capitalist world. Stalin argued that to try to export revolution would only provoke the capitalist powers into a fresh attack. Lenin agreed with Stalin and ordered Communist Parties abroad to stop agitating for their own revolutions. He told them to cooperate with other left-wing parties of the West to win control of the trade unions. If the Western labor movement could be made pro-Soviet, the capitalist nations would be powerless to attack Russia.

Suddenly, In April, 1922, Lenin suffered a paralytic stroke. Stalin's first reaction was one of genuine dismay, but his grief swiftly gave way to craftier speculations. Who but he stood closest to the seat of power? It was true that most Russians thought of Trotsky as Lenin's heir. But Stalin knew that Trotsky was distrusted and disliked by the Party's wheelhorses, who would keep power tightly in their own hands until someone was clever enough to win their confidence, someone "safe" who seemed no more than a modest, self-effacing broker of their wishes. . . .

The Politburo decided that Lenin should recuperate from his illness outside Moscow at the country estate of his old friend, novelist Maxim Gorky. Stalin was selected to be the link between Lenin and the Politburo, and was told to screen the sick leader from unnecessary visitors. Concealing his jubilation, Stalin humbly promised to guard their leader's rest. News of his selection caused a buzz in the Stolovka, the Kremlin restaurant where top bureaucrats ate and gossiped. Those who knew the steel mind of Joseph Stalin wryly joked that a lean alley cat had been chosen to nurse a prized white mouse.

When it became apparent that Lenin was not likely to return to the Kremlin, Stalin ingratiated himself with Zinoviev, one of Lenin's trusted intimates. Zinoviev, who hated Trotsky, was flattered into proposing Stalin as General Secretary of the Party Central Committee. The Politburo would continue to be the brains and spirit of Bolshevism, but the Secretariat would become its strengthened arm and fist. So on April 3, 1922, Stalin was elevated to this new position of power, despite Trotsky's grumbled warning, "This cook can only serve peppery dishes!"

With quiet craft, Stalin began to replace personnel in the Party machine with old cronies from his Baku and Tsaritsyn days. He was also clever in gradually reversing the processes of power, so that the Secretariat unobtrusively began to initiate new rulings, while the Politburo grew accustomed to a rubber-stamp role. All during this watchful bid for power, Stalin assumed the guise of a quiet, unambitious man who always listened with respectful interest to the complaints and opinions of others. "He did not confide his innermost thoughts to anybody," observed his secretary, B. Bazhanov. "Only very rarely did he share his ideas and impressions with his closest associates. He possessed in a high degree the gift for silence, and in this respect he was unique in a country where everybody talked far too much."

Of the five members of the Politburo—Lenin, Trotsky, Zinoviev, Kamenev and Stalin—Trotsky was the best known to the

Russian public after Lenin; Stalin perhaps the least. It was galling to Stalin to hear Trotsky constantly hailed by crowds as the hero of the Revolution, while he remained a vague, obscure figure in the background known only to Party workhorses. He wrote peevishly, "There are men, leaders of the proletariat, who are not talked about in the press, perhaps because they are not fond of talking about themselves, but who are nevertheless the vital sap and the authentic leaders of the Revolution!"

He fought Trotsky the only way he knew how—stealthily building a secret network of tough Party officials who trusted Stalin the man of action, and were pledged to follow him. He bided his time patiently. His talent for waiting had been sharpened by long tedious years in prison and in exile.

To tighten his control of local and regional political machinery, he instructed the Cheka, that Russian version of the FBI, to develop secret files on almost half a million Party officials and members. "It is necessary to study every worker through and through in every detail," he told Dzerzhinsky. The files helped him block advancement to all supporters of Trotsky and purge all Party members overheard speaking against Stalin, while promoting his own followers.

When Trotsky discovered what Stalin was doing behind the facade of routine Party drudgery, he protested indignantly. Stalin calmly pointed out that Trotsky's authority as a Politburo member extended only to matters of high policy, while the General Secretariat had charge of Party personnel and organization. The rest of the Politburo, irritated by Trotsky's arrogant manner, supported Stalin.

As his power increased, Stalin showed himself ruthless in rooting out inefficiency in the Russian civil service system. When the railroads failed to bring Siberian grain to the hungry Volga region, he appointed a new Commissar of Railroads—Dzerzhinsky. The Cheka chief went to western Siberia to investigate. When he was ready to return, Dzerzhinsky had to send four cables to Omsk, capital of the republic, before he could finally get a train sent to pick him up. Arriving in Omsk in the middle of the night, he at once called a mass meeting of the whole west Siberian railroad administration from the chief official down. He asked quietly what had happened to the first three cables he had sent. A frightened clerk confessed he had simply filed them for reference, not realizing at first who Dzerzhinsky was. The head of the Cheka ordered the chief official and all his department heads, plus the cable clerk, into the adjacent courtyard, where they were shot. Appointing new officials on the spot, Dzerzhinsky said blandly, "I would suggest a higher order of efficiency here. The Secretary General and I will expect regular shipments of grain in the trains from Omsk from now on. On schedule!" They were.

Stalin saw nothing immoral in the use of terror. Swift, ruthless action was justified, he felt, because many lives might be saved later by the prompt removal of a saboteur of the Revolution. Secret arrests in the dead of the night were especially valuable because of the terror they struck in the hearts of those tempted to betray Socialism. A typical example of early Communist justice was the execution of five hundred former nobles, landlords, and bankers, on the same night of an unsuccessful attempt to assassinate Lenin in Moscow.

Walter Duranty once reproached a Scottish Communist working for the Comintern for condoning such massacres. "They're a hard lot, those Bolsheviks," the Scot admitted,"but when you know what they've suffered from the devils who held power in the old days, the Tsars and officers, landlords and Okhrana, you won't blame the Bolsheviks for anything they have done!"

At first Stalin had Lenin's complete support and trust during Stalin's visits to the Gorky estate to keep him posted on current events. But Lenin became suddenly furious upon questioning Dzerzhinsky and learning about Stalin's brutal methods in suppressing the Georgian independence movement. During a visit from Kamenev, Lenin angrily denounced Stalin for having disgraced the regime by using Tsarist tactics as Secretary General. Kamenev warned Stalin privately, "Lenin is preparing to reverse your nationalities policy."

Stalin's heart beat faster as he stammered, "In my opinion, firmness is necessary against Lenin!" It was the first daring defiance of his lifelong idol. Stalin's shrewd peasant instincts warned him that his career was suddenly approaching a crisis. He had reached a point of no return, and the road ahead was a desperate one. The pupil could either allow himself to be crushed and discarded by the master whose favour he had lost; or he could challenge and overthrow the master.

He steeled himself to take the dangerous chance.

7

Kremlin Struggle for Power

Stalin began to clash with Lenin over how much independence should be given to the outlying republics. He insisted that nationalism could be curbed only by strict control from Moscow, but finally agreed to a reorganization of the government as a "voluntary" Union of Soviet Socialist Republics (USSR). American correspondents, amazed at the new Constitution that allowed each republic the right to secede, questioned Stalin about it.

"Naturally, we don't mean it for the *present* Soviet Republics," he explained, "but for territories like that of England, Germany or America if they eventually decide to join the USSR." They couldn't decide whether he was pulling their leg.

Lenin suffered a second stroke on December 16, 1922, making it clear he could never again return to the Kremlin. His place was promptly taken by a triumvirate—Zinoviev, Kamenev and Stalin, with Molotov, Bukharin and Kalinin as their deputies. Trotsky was significantly excluded. During his visits to Lenin, Stalin grew more and more evasive about what was going on, but Krupskaya, Lenin's wife, warned him about the bureaucratic machine Stalin was secretly building, his brutality toward defiant nationalities, his spiteful behaviour toward personal enemies. Sickened, Lenin made up his mind that Stalin was simply not fit to be trusted with so much power. He wrote to Trotsky asking him to join forces against Stalin.

One of Stalin's spies brought him a copy of the letter. Furious, he telephoned Krupskaya under the pretext of asking about Lenin's health. Losing his temper, he snarled at her for bothering her husband with Party gossip, even cursing her and threatening to bring her to trial before a Party commission. Krupskaya, already worried and exhausted by her long ordeal of caring for the man she had loved devotedly all her life, almost collapsed from the shock. She wrote an anguished note to Kamenev, chairman of the Politburo: "I beg you to protect me from rude interference with my private life and from vile invectives and threats." Lenin fell into so great a fury at Stalin that he suffered another stroke, which paralyzed his right arm and leg.

But he still grimly insisted upon dictating a political last will and testament to one of his secretaries, in the form of "A letter to the Congress." It was to be kept absolutely secret until the Party Congress met in three months. "Having become General Secretary, Comrade Stalin has concentrated boundless power in his hands," he charged, "and I am not certain he can always use this power with sufficient caution. On the other hand, Comrade Trotsky . . . is, I think, the most able person in the present Central Committee." Five days later he added a blunter postscript: "Stalin is too rude, and this fault . . . becomes unbearable in the office of General Secretary. Therefore I propose to the comrades to find a way to remove Stalin from that position and appoint to it another man . . . more patient, more loyal, more polite and more attentive to comrades, less capricious, etc." He also warned that failure to remove Stalin would create a dangerous conflict between Stalin and Trotsky that could plunge Russia into turmoil.

In January, 1923, Lenin decided not to wait for the Party Congress and sent a series of five articles to *Pravda* criticizing Stalin openly for botching his job as head of Rabkrin.

Stalin knew he was in great danger. Spies had reported overhearing Lenin tell his wife, "Stalin is devoid of the most elementary honesty, the most simple human decency!" His secretary told Trotsky, "He wants to come out openly against Stalin before the whole Party. He is preparing a bombshell!" Studying these reports from his spies, pipe clenched grimly between his teeth, Stalin became morose, brooding over how best to save himself, snarling at those around him. Krestinsky, a Trotsky supporter, described him during this period as "an ugly creature with his yellow eyes."

Thinking fast, Stalin sought to neutralize Trotsky's opposition by a fawning proposal that Trotsky should take Lenin's place in addressing the new Party Congress. Sensing a trap, Trotsky refused and the honour fell to Zinoviev. Stalin continued to court Trotsky's good will, making meek and respectful concessions to his opinions. He also published an essay in *Pravda* singing Lenin's praises. He gave every appearance of being a chastened, humble Party official who had learned his lesson and his place. When Lenin wrote him demanding a belated apology to Krupskaya for his rudeness, Stalin hastily dispatched an almost cringing letter of abject regret.

But behind the scenes Stalin stealthily formed a cabal with Zinoviev as front man, Kamenev as strategist, and himself as organizer, to capture the Party Congress. They agreed to keep "that ex-Menshevik snob" Trotsky from succeeding to the mantle of Lenin, despite their recognition that he was the most eminent man on the Central Committee. Stalin fed their animosity toward Trotsky as an outsider, reminding them of Gorky's judgment: "He is not one of us—with us, but not one of us."

Zinoviev saw himself as Lenin's heir apparent, but he was swiftly disillusioned when the Twelfth Congress met on April 23rd in a hall packed to the rafters with delegates pledged to Stalin. The political machine Stalin had built in secret was beginning to come into the open. The hall rocked with applause at his cynical reply to a delegate who demanded more freedom of discussion: "The Party, my friend, is no debating society.

Russia is surrounded by the wolves of imperialism. To discuss all important matters in twenty thousand Party cells would be to lay all one's cards before the enemy." Trotsky shuddered at Stalin's hypocrisy in telling the Congress sadly, "I am only sorry that Comrade Lenin cannot be here himself." Lenin now lay in bed paralyzed, speechless, infuriated.

Soon afterward, forty-six prominent Party members dared to sign a Trotsky petition to remove Stalin as General Secretary; Trotsky flourished it at a Politburo session, charging that Stalin's leadership was ruining the country. Meeting with contemptuous silence, he stalked out of the room. Shortly afterwards he fell so ill that he was ordered by physicians to the sunny Caucasus for his health.

On January 21, 1924, the father of the Russian Revolution— Vladimir Ilyich Lenin—died. The news came as a stunning shock to all of Russia because few had been told how serious his illness really was. The Russians felt a deep sense of personal loss and grief for the man they felt had liberated them from Tsarism. A distant friend of Lenin's, Sun Yat-sen, the great founder of modern China, spoke for both Russians and Chinese when he said sadly, "Lenin was so strong and big in our eyes, we refused to believe death itself could conquer him."

Stalin's own emotions churned in a maelstrom of ambivalent feelings. Despite his relief at escaping Lenin's wrath, he felt pangs of grief at the loss of his boyhood idol, the fountainhead of his Marxist learning, the master he had served for over twenty years, the comrade with whom he had toppled an empire. But he could not long afford to be bemused by nostalgic memories. The seat of power was empty, and the man closest to it was Joseph Stalin. If he played his cards well, the son of a Georgian cobbler might soon become the uncrowned emperor of all the Russias.

Trotsky later spitefully raised the question of whether Stalin might possibly have poisoned Lenin, recalling that a year before

Lenin died he had asked Stalin for poison, planning to commit suicide if recovery was hopeless. Stalin had reported this request to the Politburo. There is valid evidence, however, that Lenin died of natural causes.

But Stalin was not above craftily using Lenin's corpse to advance his own fortunes. He stage-managed ornate, elaborate funeral ceremonies that would have appalled the unpretentious Lenin, rudely ignoring the wishes of Krupskaya. She had asked the Party not to organize a pompous funeral but to honour her husband as he would have wished, "by building creches, playgrounds, houses, schools, libraries, ambulances, hospitals."

Instead Stalin had Lenin's body embalmed and placed in a glass-topped coffin and carried through five miles of Moscow's snowbound streets in twenty-below-zero weather. The procession wound into a Red Square made brilliant by torches and bonfires, through a crowd of millions held back by a thick, long lane of rigid troops. As the band played the "Internationale" in funeral tempo, the final set of pallbearers took over—Stalin, Zinoviev, Kamenev, Bukharin, Rykov, Kalinin. Making a short speech over the bier, Stalin promised the dead leader that the Party would remain loyal to his ideals and work.

For a full week Lenin's body lay in state under the ancient walls of the Kremlin, bells tolling and guns thundering as endless lines of Russians sobbed past the coffin. Having established himself as chief mourner, and therefore heir apparent, Stalin lost no time in organizing a cult of Lenin worship, with himself as high priest. He kept Lenin's waxy body, reembalmed every month, on display in a squat, red granite mausoleum in Red Square. Guarded day and night by Russian soldiers, the tomb became a holy Mecca for pilgrimages by the Communist faithful. Stalin changed the name of Petrograd to Leningrad, and proposed a Lenin Institute. He ordered schools to begin the day singing, "Lenin is always alive. . . . Lenin is within you and within me. . . ." Krupskaya's anger at Stalin chilled to contempt for his crude exploitation of "Leninism" as a new Russian religion to manipulate for his own purposes.

Trotsky's absence from Lenin's funeral had been widely noticed and criticized. Lying in the sunshine on a balcony at a Black Sea health resort while every other Communist official was trudging through the snow of Red Square in a public demonstration of sorrow, Trotsky lost his final chance to seize the scepter of power Lenin had tried to hand him. When he realized this, he bitterly accused his cunning rival of having deliberately tricked him by misinforming him about the date set for the funeral. But the truth was that he had vainly expected a summons back to Moscow to assume the leadership of Russia. His grave misjudgment in failing to put his shoulder to Lenin's coffin, or to stir the masses in Red Square with an eloquent funeral elegy, cost him heavily in Party support.

Despite Stalin's skilful maneuvers, Lenin seemed to reach out in a posthumous attempt to trip him in his leap for power. Four months after the funeral, Krupskaya came to the Central Committee with a bombshell in her hand—her husband's "last will and testament" denouncing Stalin and naming Trotsky as his choice to succeed him. It had to be read aloud to decide whether it should be made public at the upcoming Party Congress.

"Terrible embarrassment paralyzed all those present," reported Bazhanov, Stalin's secretary. "Still sitting on the steps of the rostrum, Stalin looked small and miserable. I studied him closely. In spite of his self-control and show of calm, it was clearly evident that his fate was at stake."

Zinoviev rushed to Stalin's rescue. He would be the last to disregard any wish of the great Lenin's, Zinoviev assured the meeting, but surely the four months since the funeral had shown everybody that Lenin's fears about the General Secretary were groundless. So why make the will public and hurt the Party by a needless, scandalous row? Kamenev agreed, and the Committee voted forty to ten to file and forget the will.

Lenin had been both Party boss and head of the government, but now Party leaders deemed it more prudent to divide these powers among several leaders. The coalition that replaced Lenin kept Stalin as General Secretary in control of the Party apparatus. Zinoviev remained head of the Comintern and boss of the Leningrad Soviet. Alexei Rykov was made nominal head of the government with Kamenev, who headed the Moscow Soviet, as his deputy. Trotsky, still head of the Red Army, knew that time was running out on him.

Now forty-five years old, Stalin began to emerge more and more in the public eye. Russians saw a short man—he was only five feet five—with a large head and stiff mustache, sallow and pocked complexion, jagged yellow teeth clenched around an eternal pipe, and a sardonic expression that sometimes became a wintry smile. He dressed in a peak cap, dark leather coat, soft-collared Russian tunic, clay-coloured trousers, and half-length top boots. His pleasures were few and simple—chess, skittles, listening to Chopin and folk songs, reading.

He sent his children to a plain school like the children of ordinary Moscow citizens. Zveitlana and Vassily both bore the name of Stalin, which was now the legal name of Joseph Djugashvili. But the son of his first marriage remained Jacob Djugashvili, bitterly resentful of the father who had neglected and forgotten him. Stalin finally brought him to Moscow and gave him a modest allowance, but did not install him in the Kremlin or use any influence on his behalf. Jacob worked as an obscure technician and spoke openly and so harshly against his father that he had to be banished to a provincial town.

During 1925 Trotsky referred to Stalin scornfully as "the most eminent mediocrity in our Party." Yet whenever the Politburo met, with Zinoviev and Kamenev pointedly snubbing Trotsky as they entered the council room, Stalin would approach him with a warm show of friendliness and shake hands vigorously. That did not stop Trotsky from spreading the joke about the Georgian shepherd pasturing his flock and piping a melody called "We are building up Socialism in one country!" Suddenly the thunderous voice of Karl Marx came out of the clouds: "When and where did I ever say this was possible?" The shepherd shrugged, "I'm not playing to you, but to these sheep here!"

Stalin quietly brought trusted army troops and political police to Moscow. Cannily remaining in the background himself, he artfully incited Zinoviev, Kamenev and Bukharin into denouncing Trotsky and stripping him of his Red Army command, which went to Mikhail Frunze, a Stalin man. Then, executing the will of the Politburo, Stalin maneuvered Trotsky's expulsion from the Politburo and Central Committee, dismissing all his supporters from key government Posts.

Zinoviev naively assumed that now *he* would be urged to succeed Lenin, unaware that the reins of power were already firmly in Stalin's hands. Stalin not only had an iron grip on the Party machinery, but also controlled both press and police, who prevented his opponents from holding public meetings. When Zinoviev finally realized what was going on, he indignantly accused Stalin of seeking personal dictatorship, and his charge was echoed by Kamenev. *Pravda* reported only front-page attacks on Zinoviev by Bukharin for attempting to make himself "feudal lord of Leningrad," independent of Moscow control. A showdown came at the Fourteenth Party Congress, heavily stacked, as usual, with Stalin delegates.

Kamenev angrily charged Stalin with having usurped the Politburo's policy-making powers. He was cut short by cries of "Lies! Humbug!" and an uproar swelled on cue. *Stalin! Hurrah for Stalin!* Thunderous shouts swept the hall until the smiling General Secretary stepped to the podium. "Yes, Comrades, I am a frank, rough man," he said calmly. "That is true; I don't deny it. But the Party desires unity and will accomplish it, *with* Kamenev and Zinoviev if they so desire, *without* them if they refuse!" A storm of applause stampeded the Congress, which stripped Stalin's accusers of their Party offices, leaving Kamenev chairman of the Moscow Soviet.

Defeated and furious, Zinoviev and Kamenev secretly joined Trotsky, the colleague they had helped to topple, in what soon became known as "the Left Opposition." On November 7, 1927, the trio suddenly appeared on a hotel balcony to harangue huge mobs of Muscovites marching with banners and posters into Red Square for an anniversary celebration. They were unheard and ignored in the blare of bands and excitement . . . except by Stalin's secret police. Left Opposition supporters marching by were pelted with rotten potatoes and torn galoshes. Placards calling for world revolution were torn from their hands, and they were set upon and beaten. When the three glum leaders left the hotel, a pistol shot was fired after their car.

At the Fifteenth Congress, Stalin's denunciation of the trio brought their expulsion from the Party. He ordered Trotsky arrested and deported to Siberia, along with tens of thousands of Party members suspected of supporting him. Zinoviev and Kamenev were banished to minor posts in a provincial city. A crowd of two thousand gathered at Moscow's Kazan Station to watch Trotsky put aboard the train, hoping he would tear loose from the police and make a last defiant speech. Instead he climbed in meekly, looking very remorseful.

The reason: he wasn't actually Trotsky, but an actor impersonating him. The real Trotsky had been driven to a special train waiting at a small station outside Moscow. Stalin had arranged this artful deceit out of fear that Trotsky would attempt to denounce him to the crowds at Kazan Station. Trotsky had, in fact, defied the police who sought to arrest him, and had had to be carried forcibly to a waiting car.

Trotsky stubbornly refused to be silenced, writing bitter accusations in exile that turned up as leaflets in Moscow. In

1929, Stalin furiously ordered him banished from the USSR, ominously keeping Trotsky's family behind as hostages. When Trotsky began organizing world opinion against Stalin, his son, sister, and other relatives began to disappear.

Bukharin was given control of the Comintern as his reward for denouncing Zinoviev, and Rykov remained Prime Minister. But now there was no doubt in anyone's mind as to who really ruled the Kremlin. His colleagues on the Politburo began to call him *khozyain* (boss), not affectionately as with Lenin but out of raw fear. Once one of them was late to a meeting in Stalin's bare, high-ceilinged office where he sat beneath a picture of Karl Marx. "You should not keep us waiting," Stalin rebuked him severely, "even if your mother were dying!"

Drunk with eminence, Stalin began to fancy himself an original thinker, not simply an executor of the political theories of Marx and Lenin. One day D. B. Ryazanov, an outspoken old Bolshevik theorist, interrupted Stalin by laughing, "Stop it, Koba, don't make a fool of yourself. Everyone knows that theory is not exactly your field!" Stalin's amiable dry smile appeared, but his eyes glittered. Several years later Ryazanov found himself accused of treason, arrested, and exiled.

Stalin had small use for "bourgeois scruples." He seldom hesitated to do the opposite of what he said, or say the opposite of what he did. He felt that any means justified the noble ends of making the Soviet Union a workers' and peasants' paradise. Even as he seized power from local Soviets, he blandly declared, "The Party ought to embark resolutely on the path of internal democracy." Conspiring with the Party's Right Wing, he destroyed the Left Opposition. Conspiring with the Center, he destroyed the Right Opposition. He assured the Center that when the dictatorship of the proletariat had abolished classes in Russia, "the Communist Party will have fulfilled its mission and can be allowed to disappear." But he entrenched the Party firmly in the Kremlin, an unshakable monolith.

A visiting French trade union leader asked him why there was only one political party in the Soviet Union. "Oh, but we have many parties," Stalin corrected him gravely. "One party rules and the others are in prison." He exercised his terrible patience waiting for events to run their course, studying his opponents' weaknesses. At Politburo meetings he usually remained silent, puffing his pipe reflectively as other members argued. Thriving on their differences, profiting by their views, he then spoke for Russia.

Having used Bukharin and Rykov to dump the Left Opposition, Stalin bided his time until they were incautious enough to grumble against him behind his back. At the next Party Congress they were accused of forming "an anti-Party Right Opposition." Rykov lost his temper and cried that Stalin was turning the USSR into a police state, with Cheka spies reporting even on Politburo members directly to him. At Stalin's cold nod Bukharin and Rykov were stripped of all Party offices.

Now there was no one left sitting on top of the Kremlin Wall except Joseph Stalin . . . undisputed *khozyain*.

8

Stalin's New Russia

Stalin was careful, however, to appear to the Party rank and file and the Russian people only as a modest, kindly, humble son of the soil, not as the power-greedy, arrogant Communist Tsar he was pictured in the Western press. Henri Barbusse, a French admirer, once said to him, "Do you know that in France you are looked upon as a tyrant who acts merely according to his fancy, and is a bloody tyrant into the bargain?" According to Barbusse, Stalin simply leaned back in his chair and burst out into his hearty workingman's laugh.

He pretended that he had sought several times to lay down the heavy burden of Party leadership, only to have Congress delegates insist unanimously that he remain as General Secretary. "What could I do?" he sighed. "Abandon my post? Such a thing is not in my character!" The walls of every office and shop throughout Russia began to bloom with pictures of Stalin; of Stalin at Lenin's side. Following the example of Tsaritsyn, which had become Stalingrad, local Party leaders rechristened their cities Stalino, Stalinabad, Stalinsk, Stalinogorsk. Now at Party meetings when the name of Stalin was mentioned, everybody stood, clapped and shouted, demonstrating for ten or fifteen minutes, until the chairman dared to call a halt.

In 1929, Moscow celebrated Stalin's fiftieth birthday with a huge parade. The walls of Moscow were covered with giant portraits of him; his statues and busts filled the squares and public buildings. Signs and banners proclaimed, "Stalin is our hero of the October Revolution." . . . "Stalin is the Lenin of today." Watching this glorification in Red Square from atop the tomb of the master, which had now become a pedestal for the pupil. Stalin pretended to deplore it. "This is all nonsense, Comrades," he scoffed gently to the Politburo members at his side, "nothing but foolish exaggeration." He made a careful mental note of those unwary enough to chuckle and agree. Their turn would come.

No longer preoccupied with his domestic struggle for power, Stalin began to pay more attention to Russia's foreign affairs. To the dismay of Maxim Litvinov, Russia's skilled and popular Foreign Minister, Stalin decided to mastermind Soviet diplomacy. His grasp of world affairs was so inadequate, however, that on July 13, 1928, he confidently predicted imminent war between America and England as rival capitalist powers.

In 1928, he took personal control of the Comintern, ordering all foreign Communist Parties to follow the Party line from Moscow strictly, because only the USSR could be trusted to give correct Marxist leadership to workers of the world. He had no grandiose hopes, like Trotsky, of triggering a world revolution. But if he sealed the loyalties of foreign Communist leaders to him, they would not go over to Trotsky's camp and help mount a powerful anti-Stalinist movement. Control of overseas pawns also gave him a fifth column in Western nations which he could manipulate to suit Soviet policy.

He was especially interested in the Communist Party of the United States. "When a revolutionary crisis has developed in America," he declared in 1929, "that will be the beginning of the end of all world capitalism." American Communists visited Moscow that year. He scolded them for moving too slowly and timidly. They had overestimated the strength and stability of American capitalism, he told them, simply because Americans enjoyed such a high standard of living.

The foreign policy blunder that almost wrecked Stalin's prestige as a world leader of Communism was his choice of Chiang Kai-shek, a brilliant young career soldier, to lead China's revolutionary army. He brought Chiang to Moscow, trained him in Russian military methods, then sent him back to China to develop an officer corps for the new Kuomintang army. Stalin ordered China's Communists, then led by Chen Tu-hsiu and Mao Tse-tung, to cooperate. But Chiang soon made it clear that he considered his enemy to be the Chinese Reds, not China's war lords or capitalists. The Reds sent frantic pleas to Moscow begging Stalin to rescind his order. At a Kremlin meeting of the Central Committee, old Bolshevik Karl Radek warned that Chiang was preparing to massacre the Chinese Reds. Nonsense, Stalin growled; there must be no treason to Chiang Kai-shek.

A few days later the Kuomintang suddenly attacked the Red Chinese stronghold in Shanghai, slaughtering thousands of workers, hunting down Communists, even invading the Soviet Embassy. Massacres against workers in Nanking and Canton followed. Stalin was appalled, less at the bloodshed than at the betrayal of Chiang and its shattering blow to the faith of Communists everywhere that "Stalin knows best." He moved swiftly to shift the blame to Chen Tu-hsiu, denouncing him as a "Trotskyite traitor" responsible for the debacle. The Soviet press was then allowed to hurl belated thunderbolts at Chiang as a traitor, feudalist, counterrevolutionary, mass murderer.

Surviving Red Chinese were rescued by Mao Tse-tung and led to mountain hideouts, where they lived as outlaws, dodging Nationalist troops. Mao never forgot who it was that had chosen Chiang and built the Kuomintang. Chinese obedience to Moscow had cost the lives of tens of thousands of Chinese workers. From then on, Mao vowed grimly, China would run its revolution its own way, and Comrade Stalin could like it or not!

Red China's angry split with the Soviet Union in the 1960s had its roots in Stalin's blunder of 1927.

Fearing that time for Russia's breathing spell was running out, Stalin worried that the economy was too weak to survive a full-scale attack from the West. So in 1928 he launched the First Five-Year Plan, a crash program to industrialize the Soviet Union at top speed. Wiping out the NEP system of private trade and industry, the Plan concentrated on an all-out national effort to build factories and machinery instead of consumer goods. It also eliminated the *kulak,* or well-to-do peasant, by confiscating all private farms and combining them into Government collectives, to raise food for the workers. "We have to change backward Russia into a technically modernized country," Stalin told the Central Committee.

"It's not a Plan," scoffed *The New York Times.* "It's a speculation." The editorial predicted ignominious defeat. Did Stalin really expect to change ignorant peasants into skilled machinists overnight? Did he expect the Russian people to live on bare rations, go without new clothing or housing, work long hours under dreadful conditions, for starvation wages that could buy nothing anyhow? For five long years?

Preoccupied with his vision of a strong and secure Russia, Stalin was indifferent to the cost in terms of human misery. A man of steel who had himself endured long years of suffering and privation as a revolutionist with an ideal, he saw nothing wrong in demanding similar sacrifices from fellow Russians. He was concerned only with statistics showing the Plan's success, not with workers who had to be driven into factories and mines, punished for tardiness, imprisoned for absenteeism. He ordered work quotas raised and pay scales lowered in ruthless determination that the Plan would succeed on schedule.

There was another great principle at stake—to prove to the world the superiority of a planned economy over capitalist anarchy. If the Plan worked an economic miracle, wouldn't it put pressure on Western governments from their own workers for some form of Socialist planning? The propaganda value of the Plan became especially useful to Stalin in 1929, when depression hit the Western world, creating economic chaos.

Stalin's problem was not finding jobs for workers but finding workers for jobs. He had to recruit hundreds of thousands of uneducated peasants from villages to run the new machines in the new factories, and somehow train them on the job. He ordered special honours for those who surpassed their quotas, calling them "Stakhanovites" after a record-breaking "Hero of Labor," Alexei Stakhanov. Stalin saw no irony in using the same "speed-up system"—making workers produce goods twice as fast, then cutting the work rate per piece—that he had condemned in Western nations as exploitation of the workers. He also liberated women from kitchen slavery by putting them to work building roads and cleaning streets.

The face of Russia began to change. Moscow swelled from a city of one and a half million to five million in a single generation. Stalin began a large-scale development of western Siberia, using enthusiastic young volunteers eager to make whole new industrial cities spring up on the empty spaces of the frozen Urals. Fired with the same zeal as early American pioneers who opened up the Western wilderness, as today's young Americans who join the Peace Corps, Comsomol (Young Communist Party) proudly claimed that they were building Siberia into "another America."

At the centre of this enormous hubbub of activity sat Joseph Stalin. He was pleased with the successful ferment he had inspired in the cities, but angered by the hostility to the plan in the villages. Until now peasants had been allowed to operate private farms as long as they sold their crops to the government at State-fixed prices. When the price had fallen too low, they had simply hidden their crops or sold them on the black market.

Now collectivization was forcing them to join *kolkhozes,* State farms which were virtually agricultural factories paying low wages.

Many kulaks defied Party officials sent from Moscow to collectivize their farms. Of this tough breed, Russians said, "When a kulak steals your cow, he is clever; when you steal his cow, you are a scoundrel!" Rather than turn their assets over to the State, they cut down their fruit trees, slaughtered their cattle and horses, burned their barns. Stalin angrily decreed, "He who injures the property of the State must be punished by the highest measure of social protection, namely shooting." In a land where life was cheap but property dear, Stalin considered the firing squad a just penalty for a peasant who took a piece of rope from a kolkhoz he had once owned. But any Russian who "only" murdered a comrade or two faced no more than ten years in prison.

An estimated five million kulaks were driven out of their homes and villages, which were then collectivized. Whole families were deported to slave-labour camps in Central Asia, Siberia and the forests of the Polar regions. Hundreds of thousands, including children, froze or starved from lack of shelter, heat, proper care, or bare necessities. The engineer of the Moscow express reported at least a dozen suicides every day as whole kulak families threw themselves under his train.

The kulaks waged guerrilla warfare against Soviet officials, murdering them with weapons saved from the First World War and the civil war. Stalin ordered terrible reprisals. One Caucasian village was totally destroyed by Red artillery. A particularly defiant region of the Don was depopulated by shooting fifty thousand of the fifty-two thousand inhabitants. If Stalin's steel nerves were unaffected by such massacres, many of those who had to carry out his barbaric orders were not. On the way back from one punitive expedition, a GPU (Secret Service) colonel broke down and wept. "I am an Old Bolshevik," he said. "I worked in the underground, against the Tsar and then I fought in the civil war. Did I do all that in order that I should now surround villages with machine guns, and order my men to fire indiscriminately into crowds of peasants? Oh, no, *no!*"

The Russian Orthodox Church, which had been left in peace between 1922 and 1928, could not shut its eyes to Stalin's war against the peasantry. The clergy began to support kulak resistance. Priests were arrested and exiled; churches were confiscated and turned into State buildings; Christmas celebrations were forbidden; and Stalin forbade the church bells of Moscow to ring.

The consequences of the struggle to collectivize Russian farming were harsh to a nation living on the edge of starvation. Over half of the nation's thirty-four million horses which had been used for ploughing and transportation were killed by the kulaks; so were half of Russia's sixty-five million cattle and two thirds of 150 million sheep and goats. By the end of 1932, the food situation was desperate. Grain, the Russian staff of life, rotted in the fields unharvested. Seeds went planted, ploughing was neglected, eggs and poultry were hoarded. Famine began to sweep over Russia, and Stalin had to ration food, closing down all restaurants and food shops. Now he grew apprehensive. How could his brave new cities of steel be built on the Siberian steppes if he could not feed the workers?

Stalin's enemies in the Kremlin began to find their tongues once more. "The only place in which one does not die of hunger is prison," one angry critic charged. "Every Soviet citizen has holes in his shoes and despair in his face!" There were monetary troubles, too. With goods and food scarce, a black market led to inflation. Paper roubles lost their value, and people began to hoard silver money. Stalin ordered anyone found hoarding small coins to be shot summarily.

The harvest of 1932 proved one of the worst in Russian history. Stalin wrathfully accused peasants on the kolkhozes of deliberate sabotage, and ordered the entire crop seized from any collective that had not met its quota. During the winter of 1932–33, millions of peasants starved to death.

Secret memos urging that Stalin be replaced as Party Secretary began to circulate in the Kremlin. His spies ferreted out the malcontents for him, and he demanded of the Central Committee that they be put to death for treason. But for once the Committee balked. Stalin fell into an ugly, dangerous mood. All would soon learn who was the real ruler of Russia!

He was given no peace at home, either. His mother-in-law, the widow Alliluyev, had been born a peasant and felt the sufferings of the countryside keenly. She badgered Stalin about his persecution of the kulaks until his nerves snapped and he ordered her out of his household. Nadya was shocked and dismayed, her devotion to her husband shaken.

On the night of November 7, 1932, a silent Stalin and Nadya went to a gathering at the home of Kliment Voroshilov, Commissar for Defence. During a conversation on Party policy, Nadya suddenly stunned Politburo members by openly deploring the famine and discontent in Russia, declaring that the campaign of terror against the kulaks had seriously damaged Party prestige. Stalin turned white. First the kulaks had dared to defy him, then the church, then Politburo members, then the Central Committee, and now—in front of everyone— his own wife! Glowering with rage, he burst into a violent and abusive tirade against Nadya, his voice thundering through the shocked silence of the room. Nadya burst into tears and fled.

The following day a stunned Moscow read in the press a terse news item that Nadya Stalin had died suddenly "after a long illness." A furor of speculation raced through the Kremlin, opinion divided between whether Stalin had shot Nadya at home in a dark rage at her "disloyalty," or whether she had been driven to suicide out of shame and despair. To silence gossip, Nadya was given an important State funeral, with a beautiful white marble statue erected above her grave.

Whatever the truth, Nadya's death plunged Stalin into genuine grief. Lines of suffering aged his leathery face as he marched gloomily behind her coffin to the cemetery of the Convent of the New Virgins. Without Nadya, the only person in the world he felt close to or trusted, he felt lonely, despondent, perhaps even guilty. One morning, he rose listlessly at a Politburo meeting and offered his resignation.

"Maybe I have, indeed, become an obstacle to the Party's unity," he sighed. "If so, Comrades. I am ready to efface myself." The members of the Politburo stared at each other incredulously. Was this another crafty Stalin trick to smoke out any unwary officials against him? No one dared be the first to bell the cat. Finally Molotov muttered, "Stop it, stop it. You have the Party's complete confidence."

Stalin's determination to modernize the USSR swiftly at all costs was inspired in part by a deep hatred for Russian backwardness. "The backward are always beaten," he warned plan officials. "We don't want to be beaten. The history of old Russia is a history of defeats due to backwardness."

Stalin loathed the kind of bureaucratic sloth exhibited by the chairman of one Soviet district. Stalin asked him how he was getting on with the sowing. "We have mobilized the sowing, Comrade Stalin." And so? "We have gone into the question energetically!" And so? "There is a change for the better, Comrade Stalin. We shall soon see a change for the better."

"Yes," Stalin roared, "but *how much headway have you made with the sowing?*" . . ." Oh, well, for the *moment* we can't do anything about sowing, Comrade Stalin!"

Halfway through the First Five-Year Plan it began to dawn on Stalin that Nadya had been right. Not only had the Terror against the kulaks provoked a food crisis, but it had also hurt

Party morale and cast him in the image of a bloody tyrant. Russians joked about: a bull that stubbornly blocked the road to Stalin's car until he whispered something in the bull's ear, whereupon it fled. Asked to explain, Stalin shrugged, "I just said, 'Come, Comrade bull, I'll take you to a nice collective.'"

Worried, Stalin decided to shift the blame for having gone too far too fast too recklessly, as a prelude to softening collectivization. In an article called "Dizzy with Success," he denounced the Central Committee and over-zealous local Party officials for "abominable, criminal, and exceptionally brutal conduct toward the peasants." He chided, "Collective farms cannot be set up by force. To do so would be stupid and reactionary." He called for a halt to such excesses as removing bells from churches and socializing henhouses. Furious at being made the scapegoats, some Committee members dared remind Stalin to his face that *he* had ordered and signed the Terror laws. To soothe them he issued a second statement explaining that the Committee also wanted an end to kulak persecution.

At a Party Congress on January 11, 1933, Stalin admitted that there had been serious mismanagement of the collective program, and announced a whole series of new reforms. Kolkhoz peasants would be allowed to keep and divide half the profits, and could raise and sell food on small household plots. Every village, moreover, was to have its own theatre, sports grounds, clubs, library, and cinema. Many astonished and joyful peasants were convinced that Stalin could not really have known about the terrible crimes committed in his name.

Relief was also promised for the harsh life in the cities, where whole families lived in single rooms, sharing a common bathroom and kitchen with other families; where factory shifts were continuous, night and day, with no day of rest; where women were forced to do men's work; where dancing and entertainment of all kinds were forbidden as time-wasting. Despite Stalin's blunders and inhuman cruelty, he drove Russians to inhuman cruelty, he drove Russians to accomplish in one generation the work of ten. His swift development of machines, factories, trained machinists, electric power, and large-scale farming created a new Russia strong enough to beat off the most powerful invading army ever thrown against any nation in world history.

While Stalin was busy wiping out kulak resistance, he received a distinguished English visitor to Moscow, playwright George Bernard Shaw. The Russian dictator, Shaw found, was "charmingly good-humored—no malice in him." He said afterward, "You have only to meet the Russian bogeys face to face to find out they are harmless and beneficent spirits."

Two weeks later Stalin initiated a new wave of terror that murdered or enslaved another seven million Russians.

9

The Moscow Trials

In announcing a Second Five-Year Plan in 1933, Stalin carefully sweetened the pill. Now that they had heavy machinery, he declared cheerfully, Socialism had been achieved in the USSR. Now they must use it to multiply production so fantastically that there would be more than enough of everything for everybody, so they could enjoy *Communism*—when everyone could help himself to whatever he needed!

Gaiety was encouraged under a new Stalin slogan, "Life has become easier and more cheerful!" Workers were given every sixth day off. Restaurants were reopened, some staging fashion shows for officials' wives. Factories held classes in modern dance steps—attendance compulsory. One summer night in 1934, walking with colleagues near his summer residence in the Caucasus, Stalin watched people dancing to a jazz band in a hotel pavilion. "Enjoying themselves," he chuckled. "Very good."

In just five short years he had amazed the Western world by transforming a backward, despised Russia into a modern industrial society. Now, he mused, why couldn't he use the next five years to change his uncouth, ignorant people into cultured citizens the equal of any in the world?

"I want to talk about people," he told the graduating class of Frunze Academy, Russia's West Point. "Comrades, the slogan 'machines decide everything' reflects a period now past. It must be replaced by a new slogan—'people decide everything.' Now is the time to realize that, of all the valuable capital the world possesses, the most valuable is people."

He began a campaign of *kultura* (culture) to teach every Russian to read and write, along with instructions in hygiene, etiquette, and well-bred behaviour. Girls were encouraged to use lipsticks and carry handkerchiefs. Men were ordered to dress neatly, behave politely, speak courteously. Scolded as *nekulturny* (uncultured) were boys who spoke roughly to girls, girls who behaved loosely, fathers who beat sons, peasants who cursed, soldiers who shoved civilians.

To give these new Russians an inspiring symbol of their new Soviet, Stalin built the world's most beautiful subway, the Moscow underground. Its palatial passages, gleaming with marble columns, semiprecious stones, mosaic floors, and beautiful sculptures quickly became the showplace of the Soviet Union, a source of wonder and national pride to all Russians. Confiscated churches changed overnight from "State Antireligious Museums" to "Museums of Religious Cultural History," with all church-baiting signs and pamphlets removed.

Was this a new, kindlier, mellower Stalin? Was it true, after all, that he had indeed been innocent of the slaughter of the kulaks, deceived by bloodthirsty subordinates?

The answer was not long in coming.

When the Bolsheviks had first won power, Lenin, knowing that conspiracy came as naturally to them as breathing, had made each Party leader pledge never to kill a rival or have him assassinated. That pledge was kept for sixteen years until December 1, 1934, when Sergei Kirov was murdered. He was the young, popular Party chief of Leningrad, considered Stalin's close friend and probable successor. The Politburo, which credited Kirov with talking Stalin into the liberal reforms of 1933, wanted him to join them in the Kremlin. Stalin began to suspect a plot to replace him with Kirov. A few days before Kirov was scheduled to arrive in Moscow, he was assassinated.

Stalin rushed to Leningrad to take personal charge of the investigation. He displayed great public grief and indignation, even kissing the corpse. Grilling the assassin himself, Stalin angrily announced that he had confessed belonging to a group of young terrorists loyal to Zinoviev. Stalin flew into a great public rage at Henry Yagoda, new head of his secret police (now called GPU), for failure to discover the plot. George F. Kennan, former US Ambassador to the Soviet Union, later wrote, "There is every probability, in the light of the evidence now available, that it was Stalin himself who inspired the murder of his Number Two in the Party."

Nevertheless, Stalin was apparently stunned to discover a genuine opposition group of armed Leningrad youths embittered by the First Five-Year Plan. He promptly ordered 117 suspects shot without trial as "White Guard Terrorists." Thousands of Leningrad Party members, many followers of Kirov, were exiled to Siberia. Zinoviev and Kamenev were taken from prison, accused of inspiring the plot and held for secret trial.

Shocked, Maxim Gorky, the great Russian writer and Stalin's friend, tried to persuade him that there was really no serious conspiracy against him. But Stalin seemed wholly irrational and obsessed with dark notions, a state of mind Gorky had observed in him ever since Nadya's death. He may have been suffering from neurotic suspicion, with delusions of persecution based on twisted logic—paranoia.

Returning from Leningrad, he surrounded the Kremlin with GPU officers and gave every Politburo member, including himself, a bodyguard. Anyone who lingered in Red Square was now swept into a GPU office, searched for weapons and questioned. Ammunition was forbidden to troops during parades. Anyone visiting the Kremlin on business had to follow an exact route indicated on his pass. Stalin's movements were kept secrets of state.

He was bemused by news out of Germany on June 30, 1934, that Adolf Hitler had suddenly instituted a "Blood Purge5' of the Nazi Party, killing off Party members he no longer trusted. When Stalin asked other Bolshevik leaders what they thought of this, all agreed it would seriously weaken the Nazi regime.

"No," Stalin disagreed. "Hitler has strengthened it. Bloodletting is a necessary part of political doctoring." His thoughtful look sent a cold chill down Politburo spines.

The year 1935 began a period of Soviet history strikingly similar to the Jacobin rule by guillotine at the end of the French Revolution. There had been some purges from the outset of the First Five-Year Plan, but only on a modest scale. In 1928, some Russian engineers in charge of the inefficient Donetz mines had been tried and shot as saboteurs. In 1933, thirty-five agricultural officials were executed for such crimes as "allowing weeds to grow in the fields." But in 1935, Stalin turned the whole nation into a police state. Any Russian caught talking to a foreigner was automatically arrested for treason. Thousands of Old Bolsheviks were accused as traitors in secret trials, condemned without proof, then shot.

The Society of Old Bolsheviks, an influential group of revolutionary veterans, began to grumble against Stalin as an Asiatic despot, a new Ivan the Terrible. "He is the most vindictive man on earth," said Leonid Serebriakov. "If he lives long enough, he will get everyone of us who ever injured him in speech or action!" Spies told Stalin he was being accused of staging secret trials because his accusations were false and unbelievable. Stung, Stalin outlawed the society and grimly announced that sensational *public* trials would be held.

These took place in the Hall of Nobles, a former club for Moscow nobility. Beneath white walls draped with red damask hangings, three uniformed judges presided on a high dais. Defendants sat on chairs in a kind of jury box. Several rows of seats in the hall were reserved for foreign journalists and the diplomatic corps. The prisoners, presumed guilty until they could prove themselves innocent, were not allowed legal counsel during the trial. Sessions were long and exhausting, lasting eight hours a day until 10:00 P.M.

The first trial involved a conspiracy of thirty Party members led by Kamenev and Zinoviev as agents of Trotsky. They were accused of espionage and high treason, including the murder of Kirov and the planned assassination of Stalin. Each defendant confessed to all charges, condemned himself, accused the others, cursed Trotsky and praised Stalin.

When Stalin's prosecutor, Andrei Vishinsky, put Kamenev on the witness stand, he demanded to know whether the prisoner would describe his 1933 promise to stop plotting against Stalin as "deception." Kamenev replied miserably, "No, worse than deception." Perfidy, then? "Oh, worse!" Did Kamenev consider *treason* the proper word for his behaviour? "You have found the word!" Kamenev sighed abjectly. The Soviet press raged, "The Kamenev-Zinoviev conspirators are wild dogs, beasts, and vipers who must be shot!" They were shot. Ironically, when Stalin had expelled Trotsky from the Party, both Zinoviev and Kamenev had urged him to have Trotsky shot. But Stalin had refused, sighing, "If you chop off one head today, still another tomorrow, what in the end will be left of the Party?"

The dramatic way the purge trials were staged, with a full corps of foreign diplomats and journalists present, left no doubt that Stalin was really placing Trotsky on trial *in absentia.* He wanted to prove to the world and to the Russians that he had been right in branding Trotsky a dangerous traitor. Testimony indicted Trotsky for plotting with the Germans and Japanese to combine their attack on the Soviet Union with his revolution from within. Stalin used the trial revelations to justify the extreme measures he had ordered to fight capitalistic encirclement. They also helped him discredit anti-Stalinism in the Western working-class movements as a Trotskyite-Fascist scheme.

Stalin was never once seen at the trials, but he often sat listening in deep absorption behind curtains in the semicircular recess of a high gallery at the rear, where Tsarist bands had once played. He enjoyed the trials immensely, savoring the spectacle of his enemies—Russia's highest officials—as prisoners in the dock, squirming in humiliation as they publicly repented their treachery to him. It was a debauch of sweet revenge, much like the childhood daydreams of vengeance little Sosso Djugashvili must have fantasized against the drunken, brutal father who used to beat him unmercifully.

At first, the foreign press and diplomatic corps were wholly sceptical about the trials, convinced they were simply a frame-up and propaganda device being used by Stalin in his struggle to consolidate his power. Why should so many high Soviet officials be so eager and willing to convict themselves out of their own mouths, heaping accusations upon themselves as despicable traitors in an orgy of degrading confessions, knowing that their only reward would be death? Some observers were convinced that they had been drugged or tortured.

The prisoners themselves offered a number of reasons for confessing. Some said that the success of the First Five-Year Plan had made them realize Stalin was right, and they repented plotting against him. Still others pleaded that they had been misled by Trotsky, and wanted to denounce him when the GPU showed them proof he had been secretly plotting with Germany and Japan. So many prisoners in the early trials accused themselves, however, simply because only those who were willing to confess abjectly in public were brought into court; the others were liquidated in secret trials. Some, hopelessly implicated by the confessions of others, sought to escape a death sentence by cooperating. A few innocent defendants confessed along with the guilty, often lying preposterously, because of threats to loved ones held as hostages.

As the trials wore on, the defendants themselves—as well as the foreign observers—grew stunned by the mountains of damning evidence the government produced to prove its case.

"I have talked to many if not all of the members of the diplomatic corps here," Joseph E. Davies, then US ambassador in Moscow, reported to the US State Department, "and with possibly one exception, they are all of the opinion that the proceedings established clearly the existence of a political plot and conspiracy to overthrow the government." When two former US Assistant Attorneys-General, Charles Warren and Seth W. Richardson, studied the Moscow trial transcripts, each agreed that most defendants were unquestionably guilty.

Among those shaken by the testimony of the trials was Stalin himself, who had not fully realized the extent of the conspiracy against him. He ordered forty men of his own bodyguard tried in secret; two were executed, the others jailed. A new bodyguard was recruited from Georgian soldiers, Stalin hopeful that he would be safer in the hands of fellow Caucasians.

Apprehensive that the trials might make him seem too bloodthirsty to the Russian people, Stalin began trying to improve his public image by appearing at popular festivals to accept flowers from children and hand out medals to winners of athletic contests. He smiled benignly as he was photographed with Stakhanovite workers and peasants on collective farms "expressing gratitude to Comrade Stalin for their happier lives."

Urged by Maxim Gorky, he also interrupted the purges long enough to give the USSR a new Constitution as a hint at home and abroad that Russia's raw revolutionary period was drawing to a close. He told the Eighth Congress of the Soviets that as long as Russia was surrounded by hostile capitalist powers, as the Moscow trials proved, the State could not "wither away" as Lenin had hoped, but would have to become even more powerful. Yet a modernized Constitution would bring new liberties to the Russian people, he promised. Now every Soviet citizen, even priests and former White Guards, would be entitled to cast a secret ballot in popular elections. Of course, he added quickly, "in the USSR there is ground for one party only," since the Communist Party represented *all* Russian workers and peasants.

Yagoda, the GPU chief who was carrying out Stalin's great purges, had been awarded the Order of Lenin and promoted to become Commissar of State Defence. To his astonishment and dismay, Stalin suddenly ordered his arrest as an "enemy of the people." Yagoda was charged with a variety of crimes—conspiring with Bukharin against Stalin; poisoning his ex-boss to get his job; poisoning Maxim Gorky's son to get his wife; then poisoning Maxim Gorky out of fear of his influence with Stalin. But cynical Old Bolsheviks whispered that Yagoda's real crime, after fifteen years of doing Stalin's dirty work, was knowing where too many bodies were buried. By turning on Yagoda, too, Stalin could once again pretend innocent indignation at brutal acts of terror he himself had ordered.

To succeed Yagoda, Stalin appointed a young, servile, dwarf-sized henchman named Nikolai Yezhov, who proved even more bloodthirsty than his predecessor. He preferred mass arrests, secret trials, instant wholesale executions. In January, 1937, however, Stalin ordered another show trial. Seventeen former Trotskyites, who apparently had gone back on their word to Stalin to "repent," were brought to the dock. Called the "Radek trial" after the brilliant journalist Karl Radek, who was its central figure, it ended with death sentences for all. But Radek and three others were allowed to go to jail instead for giving secret evidence incriminating the Red Army General Staff.

In June, Russians were thunderstruck to read in the Soviet press that eight top generals, including one marshal, had confessed in a secret trial to conspiring with the German foreign office, and had been shot forty-eight hours later. German nationals all over Russia had been arrested under suspicion of espionage, over the indignant protests of the German Ambassador.

Stalin had decided against making this trial public because the generals, while willing to admit a "mistaken policy," stubbornly refused to accuse themselves of treason. To convince Russians that they were guilty, Yezhov ordered their widows to denounce them as traitors in the press. Those who refused were sent to Siberia with their children and parents.

The last great Moscow trial took place in 1938, when twenty-one top-ranking Bolsheviks were tried for treason. They included Bukharin and Rykov, leaders of the Right Opposition; Krestinsky, Deputy Commissar for Foreign Affairs; and Yagoda. Yezhov proved that they had conspired with the executed Red Army generals to overthrow the government by a *coup d'etat,* with the aid of the secret service organizations of Germany and Japan. All but three of the plotters were sent before a firing squad. There was high irony in the spectacle of Yagoda, the cruel inquisitor, marching meekly into the machine of death into which he had been feeding thousands of victims.

A visiting English MP, Lady Astor, asked Stalin bluntly, "How long are you going to go on having people shot, Mr. Stalin?" Unruffled, he replied, "Just as long as I have to." In his eyes any attempt to replace his brand of Communism with a different administration was high treason to the Soviet Union—because *he* was the Soviet Union.

Something like panic began to grip Russia. What was wrong when so many top Soviet leaders had even been willing to conspire with Germany and Japan to get rid of the Stalin regime? Government officials lived in a state of terror, dreading that someone would denounce them, bringing a banging on the door in the middle of the night. Victims dragged off by the GPU were not heard from again for months, if at all. Chief targets of Yezhov were Soviet employees of foreign trade missions and Soviet officials who had served abroad. If they escaped a death sentence for spying, they faced up to twenty-five years in jail. Stalin had stiffened the penalty from a maximum of ten because, he explained piously, it might incline more judges to send more convicted malefactors to jail instead of to the firing squad.

The Terror finally came to an end with the arrest and execution of none other than Yezhov himself, who followed his predecessor Yagoda for the same crime of knowing too much to be allowed to survive his victims. Stalin replaced him with Lavrenti Beria, a fellow Georgian and ardent admirer. All of Russia heaved a nervous sigh of relief when Stalin finally told a new Party Congress in March, 1939, "Undoubtedly we shall have no further need of resorting to the method of mass purges."

There was very little left, indeed, to purge. Stalin had killed over half the Party Congress, five out of seven Central Committee members, one out of four army officers, almost all the ambassadors and ministers representing the USSR abroad, the whole of the Moscow diplomatic ministry, hundreds of thousands of top Government officials, Party leaders, army commanders, police officials. The only old Bolshevik leaders left now were Stalin, Kalinin, and Voroshilov. An estimated seven million people had disappeared into GPU mass burial pits or into the vast slave-labour camps of Siberia.

The diplomatic corps in Moscow was convinced that Stalin had seriously weakened the Soviet by such enormous bloodletting of the nation's leadership. They reported to London, Washington and Paris that the Red Army could scarcely be considered in any shape to check the growing military might of Germany and Japan. These reports made the West hesitate about taking a hard line toward Hitler. But Stalin had been far shrewder than the West gave him credit for. Even though he had killed hundreds of thousands of innocent Russians along with the guilty, he had successfully uprooted all treasonable elements. Hitler would find no fifth column in the Soviet Union to turn the nation over to his armies practically without resistance, as he had in all the other countries of Europe overrun by the Nazis.

But the price Stalin had been willing to pay for internal security was deeply shocking to Ambassador Davies in 1937. He reported to the US State Department that the mass trials were "a most powerful demonstration of the blessings which real constitutional protection of personal liberty affords. The right of the accused to have counsel before trial, the right to refuse to testify against oneself, and above all, the presumption of innocence and the application of the old common-law principle that better a thousand guilty men escape rather than one innocent man should be unjustly condemned—all these take on a very real meaning when faced with a trial such as this."

After the trials Stalin prudently decided to destroy all incriminating official records. Letters, memos, orders, dossiers, diaries of executed Bolsheviks—all were shovelled into furnaces. With them Stalin destroyed all records which failed to exalt his image before, during or after the Russian Revolution. Soviet archives were stripped of all photos of Trotsky and other leaders who had perished in the purges. Even official films of Lenin's funeral were edited to cut them out.

To give Russians the "first accurate and reliable" picture of Soviet history, Stalin himself dictated a *Short History of the Communist Party of the Soviet Union,* glorifying his own role, rewriting history in the light of the Moscow trials, and expounding a Stalinist version of Marxism. The book became a Bible for Party members, obligatory reading for every Soviet schoolchild. Writers and historians did not dare dispute it. Jlya Ehrenburg, the famous Soviet author, later explained his lack of protest: "I did not renounce what I held dear, nor did I repudiate anything, but I knew I would have to grit my teeth and master that most difficult of disciplines—silence."

Meanwhile, what of Stalin's great archenemy . . . the man whose invisible spirit was on trial throughout the great purges, but who alone survived them? In 1936, while Trotsky was living in Norway, Stalin threatened to cut off trade relations with

Oslo if he were not surrendered for trial. Norway refused, but expelled Trotsky to Mexico, which was willing to give him asylum. Stalin grimly told the Comintern that Trotsky must die. On August 20, 1940, as Trotsky was writing his own version of Stalin's life, a fanatical Belgian Communist named Mercader, under orders from the Third International, found his hideout in Mexico City and killed him with an axe.

10

Stalin and America

The Moscow trials, as reported in the American press, scarcely made the average American an admirer of the Soviet system. Yet Stalin, ironically, continued to be a great admirer of the American system. He constantly exhorted his officials to study US methods, describing Leninism as "a combination of Russian revolutionary zeal with the practical American spirit." He despised Russian bureaucrats who were fancy talkers but inept doers. "American efficiency is an antidote to 'revolutionary' phrase-mongering and fanciful invention," he told students in a 1924 lecture at the University of Sverdlov. "American efficiency is that indomitable spirit that neither knows nor will be deterred by any obstacle, that pushes on with businesslike perseverance until every barrier has been overcome, that simply must go through with a task once it has been started."

Interviewed by German writer Emil Ludwig in 1931, Stalin declared, "We respect the efficiency the Americans display in everything—in industry, in technology, in literature, and in life." But he added prudently, "We also never forget that the United States is a capitalist country."

Once he was annoyed by a garbled report submitted to him by a Russian bureaucrat who cringed and stammered, "You must forgive me, Comrade Stalin. I am not too literate because my parents were simple peasants." Stalin snapped, "That is no excuse. Our enemies in the West do not wait to ask about our parents. In America you would simply be fired!"

During the late 1920s and early 1930s, Stalin hired hundreds of US engineers to come to Russia and apply American know-how in making the First Five-Year Plan work. The first Soviet hydro-electric plant was built on the Dnieper by an American colonel named Hugh Cooper. Engineers from Detroit taught Russians American mass-production techniques. Stalin later told American diplomat Eric Johnston, "The Soviet Union is indebted to Mr. Henry Ford. He helped build our tractor and automobile industries." Jack Calder, a Ford construction engineer, was appointed chief of all Russian construction and became a Soviet idol and legend. Scorning an office, he rode everywhere in overalls on a baby camel he had adopted, jumping into ditches and climbing up scaffolding to show Russians how to use tools diligently. Stalin ordered him made the hero of a popular Soviet play called *Tempo,* which glorified Calder as a shining example to Russian technicians and workers. Fully two thirds of Russia's biggest industrial enterprises, Stalin admitted to Johnston, had been built with either American material help or American technical assistance.

Even American writers had a hand in shaping the new Soviet economy. When Stalin read Bret Harte's novels about the California gold rush, he called on his American engineers to revitalize Russia's gold mining industry, which had shut down after the Revolution. Stalin hoped that gold would develop Siberia as the American gold rush had boomed California. The engineers also helped to open up Siberia by building an efficient railway system and developing Vladivostok. By 1938, the Soviets were enjoying an annual gold output worth about £50,000,000. "There is among the people of my country," said Alexander Troyanovsky, first Soviet Ambassador to the United States, to President Roosevelt in 1933, "a most natural feeling of sympathy, respect and admiration for your great country, which they associate with high technical and scientific progress."

Stalin's admiration for American know-how did not, never-theless, prevent him from causing as much labour mischief as he could through the Comintern. By keeping the West's hands full coping with labor unrest, he could buy the time he needed to make the USSR strong and secure against attack. Soviet foreign policy followed the wily tactic Stalin had first used as a boy—subtly turning one foe against another, while he faded into the background to enjoy the battle. All through the thirties, he strove to inflame class against class in each Western nation, and to play off one capitalist power against another. The great depression of 1929–33 provided an irresistible opportunity. Communist-led demonstrations of the unemployed in Western cities carried banners praising the USSR as a workers' paradise—even as Stalin, ironically, was urging Russians to follow the American example!

To capitalize on discrimination against Negroes in the American South, Stalin hatched a wild plot calling for US Communists to agitate among them to demand their own separate republic. When Southern Negroes showed little interest in this scheme, Stalin ordered the recruiting of masses of Negroes into the Communist Party by championing their grievances aggressively. During the famous Scottsboro case, which stirred widespread indignation because of the unjust trial of nine Negro youths in Scottsboro, Alabama, the National Association for the Advancement of Colored People denounced the American Communist Party for inspiring riots near Camp Hill that resulted in many Negro and white deaths.

Stalin kept a watchful eye on labour developments within the United States. In 1935, America's Wagner Act, sponsored by Roosevelt, gave labour unions equal bargaining power with corporations. It spurred tremendous growth in the CIO, which broke away from the conservative AF of L. in January, 1936. At Stalin's nod, the Comintern ordered American Communists to infiltrate the CIO and win leadership in as many of its unions as possible. Those unions which came under Moscow influence were often the most militant.

Stalin favored the development of a strong radical movement in America because he felt that he was its acknowledged international leader. He was far less happy about the new wave of European Socialism brought to the forefront by world depression. Fear of a rival to Stalinism which might eventually threaten his own dictatorship at home led him to make a fatal blunder in Germany. Trotsky had warned German Communists to join with Social Democrats in a United Front to stop Adolf Hitler, "or the Nazi Party will ride roughshod over your skulls and spines." But during 1932–33, Stalin ordered the German Communist Party to oppose the Social Democrats instead of Hitler's National Socialists. In Stalin's eyes, the Social Democrats were a German version of the Russian Mensheviks he had fought and hated in Tiflis, Batum, and Baku.

Why not let Hitler overthrow the "rotten, bourgeois, capitalistic" Weimar Republic and take power? Hitler's barbaric Fascism, he reasoned slyly, would only drive the workers of Germany to overthrow *him* and turn to Communism. Stalin wryly referred to Hitler as "the icebreaker of world revolution." He also mused that Hitler would pose a new threat to the West, keeping them too busy to mount any attack against the Soviet Union. And should a new world conflict embroil the West with Germany, Stalin would be in the delightful position of holding the balance of power, frantically wooed by both sides.

All foreign news appearing in the Soviet press was carefully doctored to put the West in the worst possible light. Captions under photos of demonstrating jobless US workers explained that forty million Americans were on the verge of starvation, with millions more dying of typhus. Russian readers learned that daily in America hundreds of workers were shot in labour disputes, dozens of Negroes lynched. To blunt resentment of Stalin's forced-labor camps, Russians were informed that US prisoners "on the devilish island of Sing Sing" were fed only five spoonfuls of soup a day, and were "smothered with steam in their cells like rats," a Stalinized view of steam heat. Such glimpses of life in America helped persuade Ivan, groaning under the First Five-Year Plan, that he was lucky to be living in a planned economy with work for all, however great the sacrifices demanded of him.

If the American press was more accurate about Soviet life, it was also not without bias; US readers were much more familiar with Stalin's blunders and crimes than his triumphs. Stalin refused to give any American journalist an interview during the administrations of Harding, Coolidge and Hoover, Republicans all. But when a "New Deal" Democrat was elected to the White House, Stalin became hopeful of official American recognition of the Soviet Union. Until then, he had kept himself a shadowy figure in the background, the mysterious but all-powerful Party Secretary inaccessible to Westerners, who were able to see only Molotov, official head of the government. Now Stalin began to welcome influential journalists he felt could help him thaw Soviet-American relations.

Emil Ludwig was one of the first permitted to interview him, in December, 1931. He told Ludwig that he had great respect for American technology, and considered the United States different from other capitalist powers because it had no feudal traditions, no landlord class, no aristocracy. He was impressed by the fact that American engineers dressed as simply as workers. Ludwig came away thoroughly charmed by his quiet affability, as were other journalists Stalin now began to see.

He told one American correspondent, "I was brought up as a simple Georgian villager, and I am no hand at making compliments, but I must tell you that you are just the sort of man I like." He began to learn English so that he could talk to Americans without a translator, but soon gave it up, deciding he was too old. "Besides," he told one American visitor, smiling, "I can say in English, 'The restroom is on the left, friends' which is enough for diplomatic banquets. And I don't need English to understand your wonderful Mickey Mouse movies!"

Roosevelt had already made up his mind to recognize the USSR, considering Russia far too big and important to be kept standing in the corner for punishment like a naughty child. He was bitterly opposed, however, by important Americans like Ogden Mills, Hoover's Secretary of the Treasury, who declared angrily, "The people of this country will never stand for diplomatic relations with a government of atheists and unbelievers!" Roosevelt scoffed at such views as provincial nonsense. He wanted a realistic foreign policy that would let him use Stalin's admiration for US technology to America's advantage.

Much more to the point, F. D. R. felt, was the amusing reason why author Maurice Hindus had been unable to see Andrei Zhdanov, then Party boss of Nizhny Novgorod. Hindus had been told dryly, "Comrade Zhdanov says he has no time today for an interview with an American journalist because he is much too busy Americanizing Nizhny Novgorod!"

In 1933, Roosevelt invited Maxim Litvinov, Soviet Foreign Commissar, to come to Washington to discuss the resumption of diplomatic relations between the United States and Russia. Litvinov returned to Moscow and won Stalin's consent to guarantee legal, religious and other rights of Americans in Russia, along with a promise by each side not to harbour any group sworn to overthrow the other. When the Soviet Foreign Office was asked later whether this meant that Russia would dissolve the Comintern, the reply was, "Oh, *that's* different!" Roosevelt was sceptical that Stalin had any serious intention of keeping Litvinov's pledges, but they were at least paper assurances to mollify those Americans angered by his recognition of the Soviet.

Happy in his diplomatic triumph, Stalin revealed his thinking about the new American President in an interview with British author H. G. Wells in July, 1934. Expressing admiration for

F. D. R.'s personality and character, he credited him with a brave but futile attempt to save capitalism by reforming it. "As soon as Roosevelt proceeds to undertake something serious against the foundation of capitalism," Stalin prophesied, "he will inevitably suffer utter defeat." When Wells asked if Stalin himself was going to change the world, the Red dictator shrugged, "Not very much. A lot more could have been done if we Bolsheviks had been cleverer." Throughout the interview he doodled wolves, castles, and the name "Lenin" on his note pad.

During the Second Five-Year Plan, Stalin did his best to give Soviet life an *Amerikanski* flavour. The Russian standard of living began to improve: long blocks of apartment houses were built in Moscow and the provinces; specialty shops opened, offering luxuries, gourmet foods, cosmetics; Christmas trees appeared in public squares along with a Soviet version of Santa Claus, "Father Frost." But the USSR still had a long way to go to rival American economic standards, as a favourite Moscow joke testified. An unemployed Russian widow, asked how she managed to live so well, explained that her son took care of her. Her son Boris; the engineer? No, he could scarcely support his own family. Her son Ivan, the Party official? No, he still wore nine-year-old shoes. Then where did her wealth come from? Her successful son Dmitri—the lucky one in America. What was his job? "No job. Dmitri's on relief!"

When Adolf Hitler became Chancellor of the German Reich early in 1933, Stalin warily decided to probe the fiery Nazi leader's Eastern policy. He proposed to Hitler that they jointly guarantee the frontiers and Independence of the Baltic states, through which Moscow and Leningrad could be quickly threatened. Hitler proved so cold to the idea that Stalin prudently decided to reverse his stand on the League of Nations. Joining in September, 1934, he began to court defensive alliances with England, France, and Czechoslovakia, but found them unimpressed by the need to contain Hitler. Stalin grew increasingly uneasy during 1936, when Hitler was allowed to rearm Germany in violation of the Versailles Treaty, and to occupy the Rhineland in violation of the Locarno Pact. He became openly dismayed when Hitler and Mussolini were given a free hand in supporting Franco's Fascist revolt in Spain; and when Japan and Germany signed an "anti-Comintern pact" that clearly threatened Russia.

Understandably, Stalin began to suspect that the West was secretly instigating a revival of German militarism to use the Nazis in a "crusade against Bolshevism," hoping the two threats to capitalist democracy would kill each other off. To enlist world opinion on Russia's side as a champion of freedom and liberty, Stalin ordered the Comintern to recruit an International Brigade of volunteer fighters for the Spanish Loyalist Army, and sent them arms to oppose those sent by Hitler and Mussolini. The word flashed out to Communist Parties all over the world to demonstrate for an anti-Fascist "united front" and "collective security," as being in the interests of the West as well as the Soviet. Speaking for Stalin, Molotov warned the 1936 Party Congress, "The Nazis are ready to strike!"

Stalin used an interview with American publisher Roy Howard to appeal directly to the American people for support of his collective security policy against Fascism. He assured Howard he had no plans for world revolution, branding this belief in America "a tragicomic misunderstanding." He said, "The export of revolution is nonsense. Each country makes its own revolution, if it wants to, and if it does not want to, there will be no revolution." Yes, the Soviet and capitalist systems were different, but both could find advantage in cooperation and peaceful coexistence. It was the first public statement of a vital Soviet policy that would later be championed by a successor, Nikita Khrushchev, causing a gigantic split in the Communist world when challenged by Russia's chief rival, Red China, which continued to believe with Trotsky that world revolution was inevitable.

As though to demonstrate that his outstretched hand offered a handshake rather than a clenched fist, Stalin ordered Mikoyan, then his Minister of Food, to go to America and arrange for more US products to be introduced into the Soviet Union—cornflakes, tomato juice, Eskimo Pie (popular even in twenty-below-zero Siberia). An American-style Automat was opened in Moscow, differing only in that it dispensed vodka along with other drinks. Molotov's wife came to Washington to visit Mrs. Roosevelt, explaining that she was buying a hundred thousand dollars' worth of machinery to increase production of rouge and powder for Soviet girls and cologne for the men. "Russian women can afford to pay as much for their cosmetics as can your American women," she told Mrs. Roosevelt proudly. "And our men are beginning to shave more regularly, and to use toilet water!"

One enthusiastic director of a Russian poultry cooperative received five new hundred-thousand-egg American incubators, and noted that the directions called for hatching eggs in 21 days at 104° temperature. "That may do for capitalist America," he scoffed, "but it is our Communist duty to catch up with and *surpass* America!" So he put the temperature up to 115° to hatch his eggs in 18 days—and got half a million hard-boiled eggs.

Two Russian authors named Ilf and Petrov took a tour of the United States and wrote a travel book called *Little Golden America*. Despite the usual Soviet criticisms of capitalist society, it captured the vitality and wonder of American life, describing a consumers' paradise glittering with skyscrapers, great highways, cars for workers, drugstores, snack bars, and other Western marvels. *Little Golden America* created a sensation throughout Russia, and even won praise in *Pravda*. It was Stalin's gesture of friendship and went far—perhaps further than he had intended—toward erasing the negative image of America he had been force-feeding to Russians in the press.

Yet despite such efforts to hold out an olive branch to the West in the hope of coaxing them into an anti-Hitler coalition, the middle classes of America and Europe remained fearful of the Popular Front movement. In England and France, they had been made nervous by strikes at home for high wages and a forty-hour week. As for East European countries like Poland and Romania, they were far more determined to keep the Russian bear out of Europe than to contain Hitler in Germany. Europe's military men were placing their bet on the Nazis, convinced that Stalin had weakened Russia seriously by purging not only the Red Army but the whole Soviet regime.

Stalin felt himself walking a tightrope. One slip might doom his nation to a terrible and costly war which could destroy both Russia and Socialism. He began to flirt first with one side, then the other, trying to keep the West and Germany from forming a solid anti-Communist bloc against him. He became especially cynical about the British, seeing little to choose between their brand of capitalism and Germany's.

"Hitler's might even be preferable," he told the Politburo acidly. "It's capitalism without democratic hypocrisy." He began to deal with America and Europe like a cunning and crafty Asiatic bandit—calm, patient and logical at times, paranoiacally suspicious at others. He grew more and more convinced that the only morality that mattered was patriotism; the only goal that counted—national survival.

In 1937, a personal sorrow intruded into his international worries. At the age of seventy-eight, his mother Catherine died in Tiflis, where she had spent her last years in a modest apartment. Long before he had brought her to join him in Moscow, where, dressed in the khaki tunic, trousers and boots of a peasant soldier, he lived and worked in a simply furnished little house inside the Kremlin walls. They had eaten plain meals sent in from a nearby restaurant, slept in bare bedrooms with plain iron bedsteads.

But even this Spartan life in the Kremlin had been too grand and bleak for a modest peasant woman like *Babushka Katya,* as she was called, and she had returned to her native Caucasus to end her days there in the sunshine.

Interviewed by a journalist who asked how she felt about having a son who had become lord of all the Russians, ruling one sixth of the earth as an absolute despot, she had sighed, "Sosso was always a good boy, but I must admit I'm disappointed that he didn't become a priest."

Millions of Russians who had lost sons, parents, relatives, and friends in the dreadful purges of the thirties probably shared Babushka Katya's wistful disappointment.

11

Desperate Chess Game

By intervening in Spain on the side of the Loyalists, who had become a world symbol of embattled democracy, Stalin was able to blur the image of himself as a bloodthirsty tyrant wallowing in the mass murders of the purges. But he limited the number of Russians he sent to Spain for fear they might become infected by the Loyalist fervour for freedom, and bring back to the Soviet Union the seeds of an anti-Stalin revolt.

When Madrid finally fell to Franco, and Hitler began withdrawing his forces from Spain, Stalin watched warily for signs of a new Fascist thrust to the east. He urged Ambassador Davies in Moscow to press Roosevelt for a collective security pact against Hitler. In 1938, Davies reported to Washington his conviction that a Communist dictatorship was far less of a threat to democracy than a Fascist dictatorship, and that "there is no doubt of the present sincerity of this regime in its desire to maintain peace,"

Events in Europe began moving swiftly toward a climax. Hitler annexed Austria, then threatened Czechoslovakia, next on the list of his *Drang nach Osten*—the drive to the east, Germany's historic expansion policy. He told a Nazi rally at Nuremberg, "If I had the Urals and Siberia, if we possessed the Ukraine, then Nazi Germany would be swimming in prosperity!" Stalin angrily warned the German Ambassador in Moscow that he would stand by an earlier promise to support Czechoslovakia if she were attacked, and sent urgent appeals to the West for similar assurances. But Prime Minister Neville Chamberlain met with Hitler at Munich in September, 1938, along with Mussolini of Italy and Daladier of France, and agreed to partition Czechoslovakia to appease Hitler.

Chamberlain returned to London assuring the English people that the Munich "peace conference" had been a great success. Stalin declared acidly, "If any foreign minister begins to defend to the death a 'peace conference' you can be certain his government has already placed its orders for new battleships and airplanes!" Angered at being left out of the Munich talks, Stalin was now grimly convinced that England and France were deliberately paving the way for a Nazi invasion of the Soviet Union. He also blamed Western plotting for Japanese Army skirmishes against Red troops on the borders of Manchuria. Was the plan for a two-front war against the USSR?

On March 10, 1939, Stalin lashed out angrily at England and France in a speech to the 18th Party Congress. He warned that he was getting fed up with "nonrealistic" opposition to the Fascists, charging the West with "retreating and retreating" and "making one concession after another to the bandits." He accused the West of inciting Hitler to attack Russia by appeasing him and by "shouting lies" in the press about Red Army and Kremlin weaknesses, to make Russia seem an easy prey. England and France were plotting a German-Soviet war, he declared bitterly, so that they could emerge supreme in Europe after the combatants had exhausted themselves. But Russia feared no aggressor, and was ready to deal a double counterblow even if attacked from both east and west. "The Russians," he warned finally, "will not allow themselves to be used as cannon fodder for the capitalist powers!"

Ambassador Davies correctly interpreted this bitter speech as a final ultimatum to the West. He wrote to Senator Key Pittman, "Hitler is making a desperate effort to alienate Stalin from France and Britain. Unless the British and French wake up, I am afraid he will succeed." But London and Paris rebuffed Litvinov's last bid for a mutual aid pact.

He was suddenly replaced as Russia's Foreign Minister by Stalin's old friend, Molotov. The change signified an ominous shift in Soviet foreign policy, since Litvinov had been the chief advocate of a Western alliance. It was also significant that a Jewish foreign minister was being replaced by a non-Jew; the anti-Semitic Hitler could not be asked to negotiate with a Russian Jew. Across the Atlantic, Roosevelt sat watching these dangerous developments with increasing concern. Warned of an impending Nazi-Soviet deal by Laurence Steinhardt, the new American Ambassador in Moscow, F. D. R. quickly notified London and Paris, hoping to shock Chamberlain and Daladier into a last-minute bid for an understanding with the Kremlin. Roosevelt also sent a message to Stalin warning that a pact with Hitler would be worthless, because Hitler would turn on Russia just as soon as he had conquered France.

Hitler, preparing to attack Poland, sent word to Stalin that he was ready to offer not only a nonagression pact, but also a joint guarantee of the Baltic States—the guarantee Stalin had asked for. He urged Stalin to invite Ribbentrop to Moscow to negotiate the pact. Stalin did.

When Ribbentrop arrived in Moscow, Stalin greeted him with a remark intended to make light of the intense hatred between Communists and Fascists: "Well, we certainly did curse each other out, didn't we?" The Red dictator actually found himself more comfortable with an avowed enemy than he did with alleged friends; at least he knew where he stood. He and Ribbentrop exchanged diplomatic lies. Ribbentrop assured him that the Anti-Comintern Pact had not really been directed against Russia, but only against the Western democracies. Stalin obligingly chuckled that the pact had "frightened only the British financiers and shopkeepers," and blandly proposed a toast to Hitler's health. The Nazi-Soviet nonaggression pact was signed on August 24, 1939, and contained secret agreements that western Poland would fall to Germany, while Stalin would have a free hand in eastern Poland. "The Soviet Union takes this pact very seriously," Stalin told Ribbentrop in parting. "I can guarantee on my word of honor that the Soviet Union will not betray its new partner." The unspoken message to Hitler was, "You can trust me—but can I trust you?"

News of the pact fell like a bombshell in Western capitals. London and Paris issued outraged denunciations of Stalin, ignoring the fact that they had turned their backs on his pleas for an alliance. In appeasing Hitler to turn him in the opposite direction, Stalin was doing exactly what they themselves had done at Munich. If Stalin now sealed the doom of Polish independence, Chamberlain and Daladier had earlier sold Austria and Czechoslovakia into Nazi bondage.

On September 1, 1939, one week after the pact, Hitler attacked Poland without a declaration of war, defying England's pledge to go to the aid of the Poles if they were invaded. England and France now had no choice but to declare war on Germany. World War II had begun, with Stalin jubilant that he had turned the tables on the capitalist powers, who were now fighting each other instead of him. But his bombshell had been hurled at terrible cost to Soviet prestige. Liberals in every country were stunned and appalled by his willingness to lie down in the same gutter as Adolf Hitler, to become a partner of Fascism.

After following the anti-Nazi Moscow line passionately for six years, foreign Communist Parties were thrown into utter chaos, their followers disillusioned and disenchanted. In America, where the *Daily Worker* had been exhorting "collective security against the Hitler beast" on the very day that Stalin was signing the pact, Communist leader Earl Browder had the thankless task of explaining why US Communists must no longer attack Fascism but only the "US-British imperialists." Marxist "dialectical materialism," they were told, required them to change their minds, slogans and tactics overnight, to reflect the changing political situation. After all, whatever safeguarded Communism in the Soviet Union benefited the working class everywhere, didn't it?

Disgusted intellectuals quit the Party by the thousands, refusing to be Kremlin pawns in a power struggle. Liberals in the American League for Peace and Democracy, a united front group, refused to abandon their anti-Fascist policy; the League broke up in angry fights between liberal and Communist members. Uneasy comrades were reminded of Lenin's observation that "each time the express train of Socialism roars around a curve, more intellectuals are thrown off." But the American Communist Party was so unsuccessful in convincing its members to follow the Kremlin line that in 1939, its leaders were publicly criticized at a Moscow Party convention, where their failure was scathingly attributed to "soft American living."

Stalin was stung by the torrent of scorn in the Western press. He told a British diplomat angrily, "Russia has no intention whatsoever of expanding into Central or Western Europe. Those who think I would ever embark on the adventurous path of conquest blatantly underestimate my sense of realities. People who make analogies between Hitler and myself show they know nothing about politics!"

He was still smarting from world criticism almost two years later when he went on the air on July 3, 1941, after Hitler's double-cross, to tell the Russian people, "It may be asked, how could the Soviet Government have consented to conclude a nonaggression pact with such perfidious people, such fiends as Hitler and Ribbentrop? Was this not an error on the part of the Soviet Government? No, it was not! We secured peace for our country for a year and a half, as well as the chance to prepare our defences." The highly practical Winston Churchill agreed that Stalin's cold-blooded pact with Hitler had been "at the moment realistic in a high degree."

"Words must have no relation to action—otherwise what kind of diplomacy is it?" Stalin explained. "Words are one thing, actions another. Good words are a mask for concealment of bad deeds. Sincere diplomacy is no more possible than dry water or wooden iron." However hypocritical his own diplomacy had been, it had served Russian ends. He had not let himself be manoeuvred into the disastrous position of having to fight the German Army alone. And he had convinced Russians by the pact that he was trying to keep them out of the war. The Russian soldier fights best when he has to defend his native soil against an invader who thrusts war upon him, and he had a history of being invaded by foreigners.

Stalin's acts of aggression after signing the pact were understood by Russians as attempts to surround the Soviet with buffer states. If war did break out, the destruction would be limited as much as possible to non-Russian soil. Caring for no people other than his own, Stalin was now as much a Russian nationalist as Peter the Great.

When Hitler's armies invaded Poland, they moved with such speed that they crossed the agreed-upon stopping point before Stalin could rush his own troops into eastern Poland. He finally did so, explaining it was "to protect the Poles in this region from the Germans." Behind the scenes, however, he sent friendly messages to Hitler. He was still highly suspicious of what liberals in America were beginning to call "the phony war"—the war of words by England and France, while Hitler's armies continued to operate unchecked and unchallenged.

Stalin set about matching wits with Hitler, watching every move of the German dictator carefully, grabbing what territory he could between them. He demanded Finnish bases as essential for the defence of Leningrad, but the anti-Soviet German-oriented Finns balked. So Stalin sent the Red Army storming into Finland while Soviet planes bombed Finnish, cities. If Hitler was peeved, the West was outraged.

Britain and France considered declaring war on Russia, but decided instead to expel her from the League of Nations, deepening Stalin's suspicion that he, and not Hitler, was the real target of Western plotting. He was also angered by Roosevelt's expression of sympathy for the Finns. He ordered Molotov to point out caustically, in a speech before the Supreme Soviet, that Stalin himself had voluntarily given freedom to Finland after the Revolution, but that America was still denying independence to Cuba and the Philippines!

The worst blow of all to Soviet prestige was the fierce resistance put up by Finnish troops, who fought heroically against tremendous odds. When the Finnish premier was at last forced to go to Moscow to sue for peace, he was dismayed by the severity of Stalin's terms for ending the war, "If I returned to Helsinki with such terms," he protested, "there would be no crowds in the streets to sing and cheer for us as there were when we left for Moscow." Pacing his office In an ugly mood, Stalin replied caustically, "Don't worry about that. Molotov and I will come to sing and cheer for you!"

Stalin watched apprehensively as Hitler went from lightning conquest to conquest. Utterly discredited, Chamberlain resigned as Prime Minister of England, and was succeeded by Winston Churchill. After the British evacuation of Dunkirk, Stalin moved quickly to take over the Baltic states of Latvia, Lithuania, and Estonia. Two weeks after the French surrendered to the Germans, Stalin boldly invaded Romania, Hitler's ally, taking over the provinces of Bessarabia and northern Bukovina. It was now clear that Stalin was putting a thick territorial cushion between himself and Hitler, who privately expressed his growing displeasure.

During August and September, Hitler's failure to knock England out of the war with terrible air attacks in the famous "Battle of Britain" blitz gave Stalin his first doubts about Hitler's invincibility. And when America transferred fifty over-age destroyers to Britain as a first cautious attempt at military aid, Stalin realized that Roosevelt was maneuver to put the full might of the United States behind Churchill's fight to hurl back the Nazis.

He ordered Molotov to attack Roosevelt as a warmonger, to keep in Hitler's good graces; but at the same time he artfully began to play off one side against the other. While he provided Hitler with strategic war materials Germany needed, he slyly ordered the Comintern to help the French resistance movement against the German occupation. He saw to it that the Battle of Britain was reported sympathetically in the Soviet press, and personally received the new pro-Soviet British Ambassador, Sir Stafford Cripps. Yet in response to Ribbentrop's urging, Stalin sent Molotov to Berlin to discuss the possibility of a four-power pact with the Axis nations.

During the official reception for Molotov, the British raided Berlin, forcing the diplomats into an air-raid shelter, where Ribbentrop continued to press Molotov to sign the pact.

"But what would England say?" Molotov demurred. Ribbentrop replied impatiently, "England is finished!" Said Molotov dryly, "If that is so, then why are we in this shelter, and whose bombs are falling on us?" Hitler tried to tempt Stalin into the pact by suggesting that they could divide up the whole world among themselves, with Stalin getting the East as far as India. Stalin pretended to consider the plan, but pressed realistically for the oil-rich lands of the Balkans, which Hitler had already earmarked for himself.

In March, 1941, Nazi hopes for a quick victory were dealt a severe blow when Roosevelt signed the Lend-Lease Act, putting America's mighty economic power squarely behind Britain. Stalin reacted by suddenly taking over the office of Prime Minister himself, and making himself Commander-in-Chief of the Red Army. The tides of war were becoming so uncertain that he felt the need for total power and control, in order to move with lightning speed as his instincts warned. He began negotiating "friendship pacts" personally with foreign diplomats.

One of the first was with the Yugoslav Ambassador in Moscow, who asked Stalin in awe, "What if this displeases the Germans, who turn against you?" Stalin shrugged, "Let them come!" Nine days later he and Japan's foreign minister, Matsuoka, negotiated a pact which promised Japanese neutrality if Germany attacked Russia, and Russian neutrality if Japan went to war with America. Stalin astonished Moscow's diplomatic corps by showing up at the railway station to see Matsuoka off personally, embracing him as "my fellow Asiatic," and reminding him, "We must remain friends, and you must now do everything to that end." When he was sure that the gesture had not been lost on dismayed Germans present, he sauntered over to one Nazi military attaché, smiled and said "Oh, well, we will remain friends with you in any event." On May 9th, as another gesture to Hitler, he ordered the Belgian, Norwegian, and Yugoslav legations to leave Moscow because their governments had "ceased to exist."

But by this time Hitler was dark with rage at Stalin's devious double-dealing, and in no mood to be patient any longer with a nation whose military strength he despised almost as much as he did Italy's. Besides, Hitler was no longer able to pay for the Russian food and raw materials he needed. He decided to assure their continued delivery by the simple expedient of plundering them as spoils of war. Concentrating about 150 German divisions on the new Nazi-Soviet frontier in Poland, he prepared for Operation Barbarossa, war on Russia, which Hitler was confident would be a quick, crushing campaign.

British Intelligence learned of Operation Barbarossa, even to the date of attack planned, June 22nd. In late April Churchill sent a message of warning to Stalin through British Foreign Secretary Anthony Eden. But Stalin, misled by his own inept Military Intelligence, refused to believe it, leading Churchill to describe him later as "at once a callous, a crafty, and an ill-informed giant." On June 13th, just after Sir Stafford Cripps had left Moscow, Stalin issued an official communique violently attacking Cripps for spreading false, nonsensical, and provocative rumours of an impending Nazi attack. A Scandinavian diplomat sighed, "Stalin understands his Russia—but that's *all* he understands!"

Early on the morning of June 22, 1941, Muscovites strolling through Red Square were startled to hear this announcement through loudspeakers: "Attention! Citizens! Shortly you will hear an important announcement!" In the middle of the night the German Ambassador had delivered an official communique to a half-asleep Molotov, who gasped incredulously, "Can it really be that we have deserved this?" Hours later his amplified voice shakily informed crowds gathered in Moscow's streets that Hitler's armies had launched a surprise attack against the USSR, and that they were now at war.

Stunned that Churchill's warning had turned out to be true, Stalin locked himself in his Kremlin study for four days to brood and think. He had finally lost his dangerous chess game in Europe. But at least, he consoled himself hopefully, his gambits had won precious time for the Five-Year Plans to build up the military and industrial might of the Soviet to a point where they could stand up against the Nazi storm.

Breaking his official silence eleven days after Hitler's attack, he broadcast a hoarse radio appeal to his people to resist the invasion not just as Communists, but as patriotic Russians defending their land . . . their Mother Russia.

12

Democracy's Strange Bedfellow

Hitler's advance into Russia began on exactly the same day, June 22nd, and at the same river, the Neman, that had marked Napoleon's invasion of 1812. Within twenty-four hours, the Soviet Union lost 1,200 planes, eight hundred of them on the ground. Stalin quickly divided his enormous front into three parts, Kliment Voroshilov defending the north, Semen Timoshenko the center, Semeon Budenny the south. *Stavka,* new headquarters of the Red Army, was established in Stalin's private office.

In his broadcast of July 3rd, he urged the Russian people to wage ruthless guerilla war to slow down the Nazi juggernaut, trading space for the time the Red Army needed to mount a counteroffensive. Pleading for a scorched earth policy, he insisted, "In case of a forced retreat of Red Army units, all rolling stock must be evacuated; the enemy must not be left a single engine or railway car, not a single pound of grain or gallon of fuel. The collective farmers must drive off all their cattle. . . . All valuable property that cannot be withdrawn must be destroyed without fail. . . . Sabotage groups must be organized to combat the enemy, to foment guerilla warfare everywhere, blow up bridges and roads, damage telephone and telegraph lines, set fire to forests, stores and transports, . . . The enemy must be hounded and annihilated at every step!"

It was characteristic of Stalin, the old Bolshevik, that he called for the same measures against Hitler that he himself had once used against his enemy, the Tsar. Only now he was no longer just a revolutionist but a world statesman leading the fight to keep his country from becoming enslaved by invaders.

"This is no class war," Churchill told the British people. "The Russian danger is our danger, and the danger of the United States. Any man or state who fights on against Nazidom will have our aid." On July 12th, an Anglo-Russian alliance was signed in Moscow pledging total mutual aid in the fight against Germany, each side swearing to make no separate peace treaty as Russia had done during World War I. Stalin was now an official ally of Western Europe, which had so recently been plotting his downfall just as he had been plotting theirs.

If it was no longer fashionable in the West to be anti-Communist, Stalin also had to swallow all his words about Western warmongers and imperialist exploiters. Now he declared, "Hitlerites denounce the domestic Anglo-American regimes as plutocratic. But in England and the United States there are elementary democratic freedoms and there exist professional labor and employee unions, labor parties and Parliaments, while in Germany under Hitlerism even these institutions have been suppressed." So much for "hypocritical Fascist babble."

Seeking a new era of good feeling with the West, Stalin banqueted English and American diplomats in the Kremlin's ornate St. George's Hall, even as German bombers flew overhead and flashes of antiaircraft guns in the Kremlin gardens blazed through the drawn red curtains of the palace windows. Stalin's favorite joke consisted of toasting Molotov, then urging, "Get up, Molotov, and tell them about *your* pact with the Germans." At these banquets the groundwork was laid for a Western aid program to the Soviet Union amounting to thousands of millions of pounds.

On July 30th, during a conference with Roosevelt's envoy, Harry L. Hopkins, Stalin confessed that he had not really expected Hitler to attack him. Predicting that the war would be bitter and long, he revealed that seventy-five percent of Russia's war industries were located in and around Moscow, Leningrad, and Kharkov, all now threatened by Hitler's drive. Then he made a statement startling to the representative of an America sympathetic but not at war: "I would like President Roosevelt to know that I would welcome American troops on any part of the Russian front under the complete command of the American Army." Behind his impassive calm, Stalin was apparently frightened and depressed by the speed of Hitler's advance through the Ukraine, and was desperate for Western military help on any terms.

The quick submission of the Ukraine to Hitler came as a distinct shock to Stalin. Many Ukrainians greeted the invading Nazis as liberators instead of conquerors. They still had not forgiven the Kremlin overlord for his massacre of the kulaks during the bloody period of collectivization. Four hundred thousand Red Army peasants deserted to the Nazi armies. Russian discipline, such as it was, depended largely upon the threat of a commissar's bullet in the back. For a while Stalin worried about the possibility of a revolution. He ordered the confiscation of all private radios, and the immediate execution of any suspected civilian traitors.

Despite the Ukraine defections, Stalin was able to get over a thousand vital factories and plants from there and the Soviet West dismantled and moved to the Urals and Soviet Asia. What he had to leave, he had no hesitation in destroying. When Marshal Budenny retreated across the Dnieper near the mighty Dnieperstroi Dam, one of Stalin's proudest accomplishments, he received a sudden field phone message from Stalin, who asked, "Are most of the troops across the river?" Budenny said they were, Stalin, said calmly. "All right. Blow up the dam."

Hitler made a fatal mistake when his Wehrmacht invaded the Ukraine. Considering all Slavic peoples as "subhuman" creatures fit for nothing but German enslavement or death, he ordered his commanders to liquidate the Ukrainians, despite the eagerness of so many to serve their conquerors. In one prison camp alone at Maidenek, the Nazis murdered and incinerated a million and a half Ukrainians, using their ashes as fertilizer for the cabbage fields. Such barbarism horrified the Ukrainians and all Russians, who fought back with full fury. Hitler was able to extract only a seventh of the supplies he won from France.

By September 10, 1941, the Nazi blitzkrieg reached its climax with a siege of Leningrad lasting nine hundred days. Almost a million Russians in the blockaded city died of starvation and bombardment. As many as fifty thousand perished on each side in a single day's battle. "A single death is a tragedy," Stalin told an interviewer grimly, "but a million deaths is only a statistic."

What the war meant to the Russians in human terms could be glimpsed in the reply of one girl asked by British correspondent Alexander Werth if she was frightened. Toiling in a roofless Leningrad munitions factory in below-zero cold, half dead of starvation, she replied, "No, not really. One gets used to it. When a shell whistles, it means it's high up; it's only when it begins to sizzle that you know there's going to be trouble. . . . Only last week we had an accident. A shell landed in my workshop and many were wounded, and two . . . girls were burned to death." She was fifteen. Death was a commonplace sight to Russian children, Werth reported.

In October, the Nazis reached the outskirts of Moscow, and thousands of Muscovites fled on foot. Hitler ordered the Kremlin blown up as a sign that Communism had been destroyed. Stalin refused to leave the Kremlin. "If the Germans want a war of extermination they will get it!" he blazed. "From now on, our task will be to exterminate every single German who has set his invading foot on the territory of our fatherland!"

The Nazis captured Reserve Officer Jacob Djugashvili, Stalin's son by his first wife, and sent word to the Kremlin that they would give him up on certain terms. Stalin disdained to reply. Although Jacob still hated his father, he refused to help the Germans in any way. After the war, he returned to Russia and disappeared. Stalin's relationship with Vassily was another matter. As a Red Air Force pilot, Vassily made his father proud by winning the Order of the Red Banner in combat at twenty-one. He rose from lieutenant to colonel, but when he sought his father's help in being promoted to general, Stalin growled, "Go and earn it!"

Allied visitors to the Kremlin were astonished to observe how many issues, mighty and trivial, Stalin himself decided during an almost endless working day. One British diplomat termed the Russian effort "a one-man war." In constant touch with all commanders in the field, Stalin personally directed all campaigns, even as he organized the gigantic removal of factories to the Volga, Urals and Siberia. Dawn often found him alone in the Kremlin, studying late dispatches from the front, or reports of spies who monitored listening devices planted in Moscow's foreign embassies. Seemingly tireless, Stalin lived and breathed the Soviet war effort, completely indifferent to his own life as an individual. Churchill and Hopkins saw him as an incredible team leader, vastly superior to Hitler in that he was also wise enough to listen to his generals.

On November 6th, anniversary of the Revolution, he addressed the Moscow Soviet, now compelled by Nazi bombing and shelling to meet in the Moscow Subway. He admitted that they had only a third as many tanks as the Germans, but reminded the Soviet that the Red Army had triumphed even when foreign armies in 1918 had held three fourths of Russia, Next day, reviewing a parade of troops marching through Red Square to the front outside Moscow, Stalin called upon them to take inspiration from such patriotic defenders of Russia as Peter the Great and even Ivan the Terrible, and Grand Dukes like Prince Alexander Nevsky, who had once defeated the Germans. Invoking "the manly images of our great ancestors," he declared, "It is not heroes that make history, but history that makes heroes!" Old Bolsheviks were stunned to hear Tsarist rulers, until now condemned by the Party as oppressors of the Russian people down through the ages, hailed as patron saints.

Stalin also sought the blessings of the Orthodox Church, signing an agreement with Metropolitan Sergei, Patriarch of Russia, that halted all antireligious activities. *Pravda* published a telegram sent by Sergei to the atheistic Stalin: I HEARTILY AND WITH PRAYER GREET YOU PERSONALLY AS THE LEADER APPOINTED BY GOD OF OUR MILITARY AND CULTURAL FORCES . . . LET GOD BLESS WITH SUCCESS AND WITH GLORY YOUR GREAT DEEDS FOR THE SAKE OF OUR COUNTRY. Sergei also issued a ringing call to all Russian believers to fight the Germans, crying, "Shame on all those who remain indifferent to this call!"

"Without any question," wrote one observer, "streams of energy proceeded from Stalin throughout the war, and that energy halted the Germans before Leningrad and Moscow." Hitler raged as his blitzkrieg bogged down in an unusually early and severe winter, for which his troops were unprepared. Stalin's defence of Moscow aroused great admiration among his allies. "It is very fortunate for Russia in her agony to have this great rugged war chief at her head," declared Churchill. "He is a man of massive outstanding personality, suited to the sombre and stormy time in which his life has been cast." Stalin began to enjoy a new popularity in the West.

His prestige at home also grew enormously. Russian bureaucrats and journalists vied with each other in awestruck tributes— "Stalin was right . . . As Stalin said . . . Our beloved commander . . . Our adored Stalin . . . The greatest leader of all times and all nations . . ." His subordinates were careful to follow him at a respectful distance, in order of importance—a far cry from the old days when Party Secretary Stalin would listen to Bolshevik grievances sitting on some hallway staircase. At the same time, Stalin was careful not to give the impression of being vainglorious or ostentatious.

He refused to take salutes alone at Red Square parades, always placing himself inconspicuously among dozens of other officials. At Party meetings, he often sat down in the back row, and was the last to speak. Spotted at public gatherings and given a roaring ovation, he refused to stand or bow, simply joining in the applause he pretended to regard as a tribute to the Communist Party, rather than to him personally. His two most extravagant vices were a pipe and a book. Foreign correspondents began to speak of him fondly as "Uncle Joe," agreeing with former Ambassador Joseph Davies' appraisal: "A child would like to sit in his lap, and a dog would sidle up to him." It was hard to reconcile this new amiable image of Russia's war leader with the bloodthirsty tyrant of the purges.

During the long winter of 1941–42, guns, tanks, and planes began to pour out of the factories moved to the Urals. Factory directors grew accustomed to phone calls from Moscow in the middle of the night as Stalin himself gruffly demanded to know why this weapon or that piece of equipment didn't work properly. Military supplies started to arrive from America and Britain in impressive quantities. When one American shipment failed to materialize on time, an apologetic US official explained that strikes were holding up production.

"How is that possible?" Stalin snapped incredulously. "Don't you have police?" The Comintern flashed the word to the American Communist Party, which promptly campaigned to replace the slogan "Strike!" with a new one, "Work!" Many US trade union officials understandably reacted with outrage.

Stalin was grimly pleased when Pearl Harbor brought America into the war against both Japan and Germany. An irony of history had made the world's greatest capitalist power a staunch ally of the world's greatest Communist power. Stalin sent Molotov to London and Washington in May, 1942, to urge opening a second front in France that year to relieve the pressure on Russia, and crush the Nazis in a vice between East and West.

Churchill replied that the British Army would cross the Channel in 1942 if this proved sound and sensible. But he added, scowling, "Wars are not won by unsuccessful operations." Molotov had greater success with Roosevelt, who said he "hoped and expected" to oblige Stalin, and approved a public declaration that "a full understanding was reached with regard to the urgent tasks of creating a Second Front in Europe in 1942." Stalin chose to regard that as an ironclad promise to him by the West, and blamed the failure of the Second Front to materialize for all Red Army reverses during 1942–43.

Two Anglo-American convoys carrying aid to the Soviets fought through the North Sea during May and June, 1942, against fierce attacks by German bombers and submarines. But when a third convoy sailed on June 27th, the Germans sank twenty-two of the thirty-three ships in a savage running battle. Shocked, Churchill informed Stalin that the convoys would have to be suspended indefinitely. Stalin protested bitterly. "This is the first time the British Navy ever turned back!"

Meanwhile, he sought to keep the Red Army intact by ordering his generals to make strategic retreats whenever threatened by encirclement. He displayed a knowledge of American history by telling a US general that Timoshenko was "my George Washington," pointing out that Washington had saved the American Revolution by his retreat from Philadelphia. Stalin called Zhukov "my George B. McClellan," explaining, "Like McClellan he always wants more men, more cannon, more guns, more planes. But—unlike McClellan—Zhukov has never lost a battle!"

The climax of the attack on Russia came at Stalingrad, key to the rich food and industrial resources both sides desperately needed. "If I do not get the oil Stalingrad guards," Hitler told his Sixth Army Commander, "then I must end this war." It was likewise Stalin's determination to make Stalingrad the decisive battle of the war. The Nazi attack began on August 21, 1942 and lasted through January, 1943. A single night's air raid killed forty thousand Russians on the second day of the campaign. The German blitzkrieg demolished block after block of modern buildings. Armed workers joined Red Army troops to fight Nazi tanks and troops in the smoking rubble and ruins. During the gigantic battle, a tremendous cheer swept along the Russian lines—American tanks and planes had arrived. Stalin's people fought with a ferocity that stunned the Nazis. Their choice was not whether they would die but how, and their desperate courage made the defence of Stalingrad one of the great heroic epics of World War II.

Churchill, meanwhile, had persuaded Roosevelt that opening the Second Front in 1942 would be too costly in English and American lives. "A premature invasion would be disastrous," he warned. They decided instead to invade North Africa, defeat Rommel's armies there, then spear up into Italy. Churchill offered to break this unwelcome news to Stalin, and flew to Moscow in August just as Stalingrad was besieged by the Germans. The meeting, attended by Molotov and US Ambassador Averill Harriman, was a stormy one.

"I find it difficult to talk about this," Churchill said grimly, "but invasion of Europe is impossible this year."

Stalin regarded him icily. "That is to say the English and American leaders renounce the solemn promise made to us in the spring?" Harriman flushed in embarrassment.

"We give you our assurance," Churchill said testily, "that the invasion of Western Europe will take place in 1943."

"And where is the guarantee that this solemn promise, too, will not be broken?" Stalin demanded sarcastically. Molotov sneered, "The British Prime Minister will then once again prove to us that his country is not in a position to sacrifice men!"

Stalin added contemptuously, "When are you going to start fighting? Are you going to let *us* do all the work? Just face up to the Germans and you'll find they're not ten feet tall!"

Outraged, Churchill lost his temper, pounding the table as he roared that only the bravery of Russia's soldiers made him pardon such rudeness. Stalin listened to a torrent of anger pour forth in rich Churchillian prose too fast for translation. Finally he slapped the irate British war leader on the back and chuckled, "I don't understand what you're saying, but I like your spirit!" He invited Churchill to his quarters for a private dinner. After several vodkas Churchill got Stalin talking about his liquidation of the kulaks. "Ten million," Stalin sighed, shaking his head and holding up ten stubby fingers. "It was fearful. Four years it lasted!"

After his visitors had left, Stalin told Molotov cynically, "They want to bleed us white. They want to prolong the war so that after it we shall be weak. But they are miscalculating. We shall not be alone—the Slav peoples will be with us!"

When the Allies landed in North Africa under General Dwight D. Eisenhower in November, 1942, Stalin was pressed for an official statement acknowledging that this fulfilled the Western promise of a Second Front. But he acidly characterized it only as a campaign that would give the Red Army some relief.

Stalin concentrated all his energies on winning the Battle of Stalingrad. To emphasize the patriotic nature of the war, he abolished the system of political commissars. "A soldier has no Socialist obligations whatever," *Pravda* explained. "His job is simply to serve his fatherland, as his forebears did." Promoting 340 army commanders to the rank of General, Stalin admonished them sternly, "Not a step back!" Now it was costing Hitler's generals as much time and blood to capture a single street of the ruined city as they had spent in conquering whole countries. Hard-pressed Stalingrad generals pleaded for reinforcements, but Stalin told his Chief of Staff, "No matter how they cry and complain, don't give them a single battalion from the Moscow front!" In great secrecy he deployed all his reserves in a huge noose around Stalingrad's besiegers. German generals, sensing danger, urged Hitler to let them withdraw, but he raged, "I won't leave the Volga! Stand fast!"

Stalin's steel trap sprang, ensnaring 285,000 Germans. Cut off from supplies, frostbitten, half-starved, wounded and without medical supplies, two out of three Nazi soldiers died in the 24-below-zero ice and snow. On January 31, 1943, General Friedrich von Paulus surrendered his remaining ninety-one thousand dazed "supermen," and Stalingrad's terrible ordeal was over.

This victory was the physical and psychological turning point of the war. Until then the outcome had been uncertain. Now the initiative passed to the Allies, and the German armies began to fall back on all fronts. Roosevelt firmly announced that the Allies would insist on unconditional surrender. As a goodwill gesture toward his partners, Stalin dissolved the Comintern in April. That summer, he mounted an offensive that recaptured two thirds of Soviet territory in Nazi hands.

Stalin's star had never soared higher or more brightly, not only in the Soviet heavens but over the whole world. Both Churchill and F. D. R. began to feel somewhat uneasy. Suppose the Red Army beat its way to Berlin before they could even open the Second Front? Would that let Stalin claim he alone had defeated Hitler, giving him the right to change the map of Europe to suit himself? Might he even sign a separate peace treaty and let Hitler turn against the West?

Roosevelt and Churchill agreed upon the urgent necessity of holding a Big Three meeting at the end of the year to unify their war effort and peace plans. "I think," F. D. R. told Churchill confidently, "that I can personally handle Stalin."

It was a naive miscalculation.

13

Stalin's Price for Victory

They met at Teheran in Iran, only two hundred fifty miles south of Baku, where Stalin had once agitated among Georgian oil-field workers. Military operations required him to stay close to Moscow, he explained to Roosevelt and Churchill. Suspicious of Anglo-American unity, he sought to keep them apart during negotiations by persuading Roosevelt to stay with him at the Russian Embassy in Teheran.

F. D. R. was chagrined to find Stalin cold and formal, impervious to the famous Roosevelt charm. Churchill was impressed by the Russian's "deep, cool wisdom and absence of illusions." Both Western leaders were careful not to alienate him; Stalin was well aware of their apprehension about what he might do, and did not hesitate to exploit his advantage. Suggesting that they get right down to business, he startled them by casually promising to join the war against Japan after Berlin fell. He won F. D. R.'s assurance that the Pacific War would be subordinated to the Second Front. Roosevelt told Stalin that the invasion of northern France might have to be postponed again, but meanwhile he and Churchill were preparing new operations in the Mediterranean. Turning chilly, Stalin sharply demanded a hard and fast date for Operation Overlord. Only that, he insisted, would shorten the war and guarantee victory. Roosevelt, himself chafing at Churchill's procrastination, agreed. The English leader grudgingly accepted May, 1944, as a deadline. Elated at prevailing, Stalin turned cheerful and offered his Western allies a few tips in strategy, such as the use of thousands of dummy tanks and planes to deceive enemy reconnaissance.

Stalin brought up the question of Poland, a sore point with him. The Polish Government in exile in London was insisting that every inch of Polish soil overrun by both Germany and Russia must be restored after the war. They were also demanding an investigation of Nazi charges that thousands of Polish officers discovered in a mass grave in the Katyn Forest were prisoners executed by the Russians in 1939. Furious at the London Poles for accusing him instead of the Germans, Stalin had broken off relations with them. Now he made it clear that he would never give up eastern Poland. The Poles could be recompensed with East Prussia and Danzig stripped from Germany. Churchill said the Vatican would certainly object. Stalin smiled contemptuously. "And how many divisions," he inquired, "has the Pope?" Churchill demanded that Stalin agree to hold supervised elections in Poland. Stalin icily refused: "The Poles are an independent people who would not want their election supervised by others!" Realizing that Red Army occupation would let Stalin call the tune in Poland anyhow, Churchill made the best of a hopeless situation and agreed to the Curzon Line, roughly Stalin's 1939 border of conquest, as the Russo-Polish postwar frontier. Beaming, Stalin assured Churchill, "We don't really want anything belonging to other people—although we *might* have a bite at Germany!"

When the Teheran Conference was over, Stalin was in high spirits, convinced that he had played his hand for all it was worth and outsmarted his Western allies. Churchill handed him a sword of honor sent by the King to the people of Stalingrad for their bravery. Unexpectedly moved to tears, Stalin bowed his head and kissed the sword reverently, Roosevelt returned from Teheran bewildered by his first experience with the inscrutable Eurasian who ruled a sixth of the world. "I don't know a good

Russian from a bad Russian," he admitted to his aides. "I can tell a good Frenchman from a bad Frenchman, a good Italian from a bad Italian, a good Greek from a bad Greek. But I don't understand the Russians!"

Fleet Admiral William D. Leahy declared, "Most of us, before we met Stalin, thought he was a bandit leader who had pushed himself to the top of his government. That impression was wrong. We knew at once that we were dealing with a highly intelligent man." But Americans simply did not know what to make of the intelligent comrade who thought like a medieval Tsar.

During 1944, Stalin launched a rolling series of offensives he called "the ten blows," hitting the Germans with shrewdly timed attacks, one after the other. Retaking the Crimea, Stalin's first act was to punish half a million Tartars who had collaborated with the Germans, by expelling them to the plains of Kazakhstan.

When Eric Johnston, president of the US Chamber of Commerce, visited Moscow, Stalin told him, "Americans will have to learn more about Russia, and I hope that you will tell them." He let American correspondents accompany Johnston on a tour of the Urals to report on the Soviet war effort.

Aware that the most stubborn US opposition to Soviet aid came from the Catholic Church and Polish-Americans, Stalin tried to soften the hostility of both to him. In the spring of 1944, he gave unexpected interviews to Father Stanislaus Orlemanski, a Polish-American priest from Springfield, Massachusetts, who had flown to Moscow to visit Polish troops interned in Russia. "Do you think it advisable," the priest asked, "for the Soviet Government to pursue a policy of persecution and coercion with regard to the Catholic Church?"

"As an advocate of the freedom of conscience and worship," Stalin replied smoothly, "I consider such a policy unthinkable." Then did Stalin think it possible to cooperate with the Pope in fighting persecution of Catholics? "I think it is possible," Stalin nodded. Father Orlemanski murmured, "All that you said is marvellous. But there's one trouble. Some people in my country, if I may dare say so, sometimes do not believe you. So what shall I do?"

Stalin looked hurt. "Why are there some people in your country who do not believe me?" he demanded. "Have I ever broken my word? If so, I ask you to name a single instance!" But he agreed to put his answers in writing. As a result Polish children in Russia were permitted to be educated by priests, who were also allowed to administer to Polish troops. Stalin's gestures, however, failed to soften the Vatican's resolute anti-Soviet position, so he angrily restored his anti-Catholic policy.

The Second Front finally materialized on D-Day, June 6, 1944, under Supreme Commander Dwight D. Eisenhower, with British General Bernard Montgomery as chief aide. Response to the news in Russia was enthusiastic. Thousands of Russian students began taking up the study of the English language. Stalin's own reaction was perceptibly cooler; he felt that the Anglo-American forces had been held back from the Continent until the Red Army had already assured Allied victory. And he frowned at the increasing fraternization of Russians with Americans in Moscow. Many Muscovites were called into the offices of the political police and ordered either to end their friendships with Americans or agree to report on them secretly.

When a Russian summer offensive between June 10th and August 15th brought the Red Army to the borders of East Prussia, Stalin knew that a struggle was shaping up between himself and the West over the political future of the East European countries being liberated by the Red Army. He was determined to tolerate no more West-oriented governments on Soviet borders. More importantly, he regarded East Europe as spoils of victory. A war-shattered Russia would recover quickly if he could exploit the rich resources of these nations by making them Communist colonies in a postwar Soviet empire.

Cordell Hull, the US Secretary of State, angered Stalin by offering to mediate the dispute between Moscow and the exiled Polish Government in London. What was there to mediate? The Curzon Line was Russia's new Polish border, as agreed at Teheran, and that was that! He handpicked his own Polish Government from Socialist Poles in Russian concentration camps.

As the Red Army speared toward Warsaw, the anti-Communist Polish underground decided to stage an uprising and seize the city, hoping to forestall Russian control. They counted on the flight of the Germans before the swift advance of the Red Army. But Stalin's divisions were thrown back at the Vistula. The Germans in Warsaw crushed the revolt, savagely destroying the city house by house in revenge. London and Washington wanted to use Russian air bases in order to parachute supplies to the beleaguered Poles. Stalin flatly refused, sending his own planes with supplies over the burning city. But by then it was too late. The shocked Western leaders privately blamed Stalin's callousness toward the Poles for the tragedy.

Stalin's mood grew grimmer as the Red Army, rolling back the Germans, discovered the ruins of burned villages, Russian bodies in mass graves, trees strung with Russian corpses. Meanwhile the dismayed Nazis were also reeling back in the West before an Allied advance that had cost half a million German casualties by mid-September, when most of France had been liberated. Six Allied armies reached the German border. Stalin played down these victories in the Soviet press, which began to hint that the Allies were hurrying toward Berlin only to share in the spoils. Stalin made no secret of his feelings, telling foreign diplomats in the autumn of 1944 that America and Britain were still decadent countries.

Churchill came to Moscow in October to do some horse trading with Stalin, winning Soviet consent to the return of

King Peter to the Yugoslav throne after Marshal Tito's guerillas had chased the Nazis out. Stalin broke the news to Tito a month later. "You don't have to restore the King forever" he assured Tito with a wry smile. "Just take him back temporarily, and then slip a knife into his back at a suitable moment."

On January 12, 1945, the Red Army opened a mighty offensive aimed at the final destruction of the Nazi armies on the Eastern front. In fifteen days the Russian tidal wave was ready to engulf the Third Reich, having swept across the Oder to one hundred miles of Berlin. Stunned, Hitler asked Goering, "Do you think the English are enthusiastic about the Russian developments?" Goering was positive that the West would grant them a last-minute armistice to let them turn and fight the Russians. "We will get a telegram from the English in a few days," he predicted confidently. The telegram never came.

With the downfall of Germany imminent, it became urgent for the Big Three to get together again on plans for the postwar world, including the occupation of Germany and the creation of a new world organization, the United Nations. Roosevelt and Churchill met with Stalin at the Soviet seaport of Yalta on the Black Sea for a week-long conference starting February 4th.

Warned that live microphones were probably concealed in his room, Churchill roared at the eavesdropping walls, "Baboons! Baboons!" Stalin, preparing to wheel and deal and jockey for position, had promoted himself from Marshal to Generalissimo. He sat between the two civilian leaders, resplendent in his dazzling new uniform, a none-too-subtle reminder to them that he considered himself the only genuinely military figure of the trio. When Churchill proposed that each Ally control a separate zone of occupation in Germany and Berlin, Stalin objected to giving France a zone. "They opened the gates to the enemy," he snapped. Churchill asked ironically, "What is the entrance fee to our very exclusive club? A loss of five million soldiers or more?" They clashed again over the rights of the Security Council of the UN. Stalin insisted upon an absolute right of veto, while Churchill protested that this might make it impossible for the UN to act against any great power that might attempt to dominate the world. Stalin stiffened.

"I would like to ask Mr. Churchill to name that power," he said grimly. "I am sure Great Britain does not want to dominate the world, so that removes her from suspicion. I am sure that the United States does not, so America may not be suspected. It is obvious, therefore, that Mr. Churchill suspects Russia of seeking world domination, and is aiming his objection to the veto directly at *us!*" Embarrassed, Churchill replied, "I am certain that as long as we three leaders who have cooperated in fighting this war are alive, there will be no danger of conflict among us. But how can we be sure our successors will remain equally united?"

"That is not the point," Stalin snapped. "May I remind Mr. Churchill that in 1939 during the Russo-Finnish war, the League of Nations chastised and expelled the Soviet Union—the same League that never lifted a finger to stop Hitler or any single act of aggression! No, gentlemen, the Soviet Union will never again allow herself to be so unjustly discriminated and schemed against in any world organization of which she is a member!" The veto stayed in the UN charter.

Stalin shrugged consent to the West's proposal for a "Declaration on Liberated Europe" which pledged to each country "free elections of governments responsive to the will of the people." He asked Roosevelt how long he expected to keep American troops in Europe, and F. D. R. replied, "Not longer than two years." With Red troops in command of East Europe, Stalin felt confident that he could interpret "free elections" in his own fashion, i.e., a choice among Communist Party candidates only. The three leaders also agreed at Yalta to destroy German militarism and Naziism to ensure that Germany will never again be able to disturb the peace of the world, to bring all war criminals to just and swift punishment. Stalin won his demand that territory be stripped from Germany in the west to repay Poland for land the USSR had annexed in the east. Big Three recognition for the Soviet-sponsored Polish Government was given on Stalin's promise to reorganize it on a "broader democratic basis."

Stalin struck a secret bargain at Yalta with Roosevelt, promising to enter the war against Japan as soon as Germany was defeated, in exchange for Port Arthur, Dairen, the Eastern Chinese Railway, and the Kuril Islands. "I only want to have returned to Russia what the Japanese have taken from my country," Stalin said piously. F. D. R., exhausted and so seriously ill that he was only four months from death, wearily nodded, "That seems like a very reasonable suggestion."

He was later attacked for having yielded too many concessions at Yalta, but Roosevelt was trusting Stalin's pledge to cooperate in maintaining world peace and respecting the right of European nations to self-determination. Just before Yalta, Stalin had publicly renounced the old Marxist idea of an inevitable clash between Communism and capitalism. He had declared, "The Government of the USSR considers that, despite the differences in the economic systems and ideologies, the coexistence of these systems and a peaceful settlement of differences between the USSR and the United States are not only possible, but also doubtless necessary in the interests of general peace." But soon after Yalta, F. D. R. and Stalin began to feud. Stalin found out that the British had met with the Germans in secret in Switzerland to discuss the Nazi plan to fall back before the Western Allies and stiffen resistance against the Russians, if the West promised to go easy on peace terms. Stalin sent an accusatory cable to Roosevelt, who knew nothing about this and cabled back an indignant denial.

As the two sides closed in on Germany, Marshal Zhukov sacrificed a million Russian troops in a fierce climactic battle to be first into Berlin. The Western armies, on the other hand, were depending on the Yalta agreement. As Churchill later admitted, "Berlin, Prague, and Vienna could be taken by whoever got there first." But he criticized Eisenhower for halting American troops at the Elbe, urging that the Allies grab and hold as much territory as possible before the Russians did. "I deem it highly important," he told Eisenhower, "that we should shake hands with Stalin as far east as possible!" Eisenhower stopped at the Elbe because General Bradley told him that a breakthrough would cost a hundred thousand American casualties—"a pretty stiff price to pay for a prestige objective," especially since the Yalta agreement required them to hand over to the Russians territory overrun east of the Elbe.

Eighteen days before the Russians stormed into Berlin, on April 12, 1945, Franklin D. Roosevelt died in office. His death stunned people around the world. None were more grief-stricken than the Russian people, many of whom wept on the streets, feeling they had lost a warm and generous friend. Stalin's concern was more practical; he wondered if the possibility of Soviet-American coexistence had not also died with Roosevelt. He ordered Molotov to attend the forthcoming San Francisco Conference, primarily to visit Washington and size up the new President, Harry S. Truman. Stalin's face darkened when Molotov reported that Truman had indicated American determination to see that justice was done in Poland.

On April 21st, the Red Army fought its way into Berlin, and eleven days later the dazed German defenders surrendered to the Russians. On May 2nd, the German High Command surrendered unconditionally to the Allies, ending a brutal world war which had cost America almost three hundred thousand dead, Great Britain four hundred thousand dead, and the Soviet Union up to twenty million dead, half of them civilians. Grimly contemplating the heavy Russian sacrifices, Stalin was determined to dramatize to his people his conviction that the victory was principally a Soviet one. At the same time, he wanted to signal that the era of wartime collaboration with the West was at an end. His plan to pursue Soviet imperialistic aims, he knew, would bring him into collision with the West, and he wanted to prepare Russians for it.

On May 24, 1945, he tendered a glittering reception to Soviet marshals and generals in the Kremlin to celebrate the Soviet victory. Proposing a toast, he declared, "I want to raise this glass to the health of the Soviet people, and above all to the health of the Russian people. I drink first of all to the Russian people because they are the most outstanding of all the nations that form the Soviet Union."

Old Kremlin hands understood this as a hint that his objectives were no longer those of Soviet policy alone, but now were also those of imperialist Mother Russia as well.

From the remote shadows of the Kremlin one could almost hear the shades of Peter the Great and Ivan the Terrible applaud their fellow Russian patriot, while the dismayed shade of Vladimir Ilyich Lenin groaned at his betrayal.

14

The Cold War

Stalin came out of the war firmly convinced that he, not any of his generals, had been the master architect of victory. Before the war the military bible of most Army chiefs of staff had been Clausewitz's famous work, *On War*. But now Stalin wrote in the Party journal *Bolshevik,* "General von Clausewitz no longer counts. We have beaten his heirs and disciples; how can we respect their teacher? No, Clausewitz is obsolete."

In another issue of *Bolshevik,* Stalin deplored the adulation being showered upon him by a "Stalin cult," protesting modestly, "It is definitely unpleasant to read that sort of thing!" He complained that the Russian people were "too interested" in him, and demurred wistfully that he had a right to privacy. For an all-powerful dictator who had not hesitated to murder several million people who stood in his way, he was curiously feeble in curbing those who glorified him. Any Soviet writer who took him at his word and tried to view some aspect of the Stalin era critically was quickly persuaded of his "Marxist error" by censors.

The Soviet Union had suffered terrible devastation in the war. Stalin hoped for a huge loan from the United States which, Roosevelt had hinted at Yalta, might be forthcoming after Japan's defeat in return for Soviet postwar political cooperation. Stalin persistently brought up the matter to every visiting American official, whom he took care to flatter. "We like you people," he told Donald M. Nelson, then chairman of the US War Production Board. "You come to us not as aristocrats, like the British, but as businessmen. And everything you send us is of very good quality!"

But important figures in the US Departments of State and Defense were hostile to offering any postwar credits that could strengthen the USSR. Along with some politicians, journalists and businessmen, they wanted to prepare for war against Communism, even advocating striking first while US military power was at its zenith and the Red Army was exhausted. One US official took it upon himself to cut off shipments of food and other supplies to the USSR, as well as to Britain, immediately after V-E Day. Truman had promised to continue Lend-Lease, America's wartime foreign aid program, until Japan was crushed and the war was over.

Stalin was furious. He told the Politburo to prepare the Russian people for a quick chill in Soviet-American relations. Malenkov made a speech explaining that Russia could not demilitarize because her "friends" would respect her only if she remained strong. "The weak," he said, "are beaten." Kagonovich warned Russians that they were now once again threatened by "capitalist encirclement."

To appease Stalin and convince him that Lend-Lease shipments of food *would* continue, Truman sent Harry Hopkins to Moscow, telling him, "Feel free to use diplomatic language or a baseball bat, if you think that's the proper approach!" Hopkins explained to Stalin that stopping Lend-Lease had been the ill-advised action of one official. Stalin snapped, "It was unfortunate and even brutal!" But he cooled off and agreed to meet with Truman and Churchill at Potsdam, near conquered Berlin, to discuss postwar problems. Truman knew that the question of Poland would be a sticky point; Stalin couldn't understand what the United States had to gain by insisting upon Polish self-determination, when Poland was so obviously in Russia's sphere of influence. He had written Truman,

"I am ready to fulfill your request and do everything possible to reach a harmonious solution. But you demand too much of me . . . that I renounce the interests of security of the Soviet Union. I cannot turn against my country!" At the Potsdam Conference on July 17, 1945, he snapped that Russia would never tolerate an unfriendly Polish Government. Churchill warned, "There is not much comfort in looking into a future where you and the countries you dominate . . . are all drawn up on one side, and those who rally to the English-speaking nations and their associates . . . are on the other. It is quite obvious that their quarrel would tear the world to pieces."

Truman had come to Potsdam with Hopkins's appraisal of Stalin in mind: "Stalin is a forthright, rough, tough Russian. He is a Russian partisan through and through, thinking always first of Russia. But he can be talked to frankly." Truman was frequently amused by the Kremlin lord's wry wit. Once Churchill opposed Stalin's request for an equal division of the German fleet by saying that the captured vessels should be sunk as "horrible things." (Diplomatic translation: the British Navy didn't need them; Stalin did.) Stalin replied dryly, "Let us divide the German ships. If Mr. Churchill wishes, he can sink his share." Once when Churchill digressed in a long windy speech, as he frequently did, Stalin leaned forward on one elbow, pulled at his mustache and interrupted: "Why don't you simply agree? The Americans agree, and we agree. You will agree eventually, so why don't you save time and do it now?" It ended the speech abruptly.

Stalin wanted 10,000,000,000 dollars' worth of reparations from Germany out of her postwar production, to rebuild Soviet factories, power plants, machinery, railroads, homes, schools and hospitals the Germans had destroyed. But Truman and Churchill stood firm for smaller reparations. Berlin was now a land "island" inside Soviet-occupied East Germany. The three statesmen agreed that it, and all Germany, should be divided into four zones of occupation, with the French occupying the fourth zone. They also ratified the Yalta plan to de-Nazify and demilitarize Germany.

One day before the Potsdam Conference opened, America's first atomic bomb had been successfully tested in secret at Alamogordo, New Mexico. Word was flashed to Truman, who decided to mention "casually" to Stalin that America now had a new weapon of unusual destructive force. Showing no great interest, Stalin shrugged, "I'm glad to hear it, and I hope you'll make good use of it against the Japanese." It was obvious that he did not fully appreciate the significance of Truman's revelation. Stalin had some news for Truman, in turn. The Japanese had been urging him to arrange terms with the Allies which would allow them to surrender. But Stalin supported Truman's demand for unconditional surrender. He had no desire to see the war in the Pacific end abruptly, hoping to attack Japan soon after August 8th in order to claim a share of spoils in the Pacific. To this end he even agreed to disavow the Chinese Reds and recognize Chiang Kai-shek as the ruler of postwar China.

Truman, who found Stalin good-humoured, polite, and extremely likable, was amused by the Russian dictator's vanity. When it was time for their pictures to be taken, Stalin swiftly compensated for his modest five feet six inches of height by moving up to the step above Truman. He also insisted that his signature should be first on the Potsdam Treaty. At an official dinner, Truman expressed amazement that Stalin could drink so many toasts in vodka. Stalin grinned, "It's only French wine. Since my heart attack I can't drink the way I used to." Such was Soviet secrecy that no one had known about his heart attack until that casual revelation. When Truman said goodby to Stalin, he said he hoped that they would meet next in Washington. With quiet irony Stalin replied, "God willing."

Returning home, Stalin summoned Mao Tse-tung to Moscow and told him to stop fighting the Nationalists, halt the revolution, and make his peace with Chiang. Mao listened coolly, nodded, and returned home seething with anger. He had not forgotten that once before Stalin had ordered him to submit to Chiang, who had promptly slaughtered tens of thousands of Chinese Reds and driven them into hiding. Mao grimly determined that what Comrade Stalin considered good for Red Russia was not necessarily good for Red China. The Chinese Reds went on fighting guerilla warfare against the Nationalists.

Stalin was far from eager to have China emerge from the war as a Communist power, offering a different Red Star for the masses of the Far East to follow. He knew, too, that historically the interests of China and Russia were opposed, and would eventually bring them into conflict. Yet if a struggling new Red China was born of the war, Russia would be obligated to help her or lose face among the world's Communists.

"We'll have all we can do to rebuild ourselves," Stalin had told Harry Hopkins. "After the war only America will have the resources to aid China." He also did not want to frighten the United States into thinking that he was trying to promote Communism in the Far East. By supporting Chiang, America's choice, Stalin hoped to be permitted a voice in the rule of postwar Japan and perhaps gain control of Siberia's southeastern neighbour, Korea, which Japan had built up industrially.

Truman, meanwhile, debated with his military, scientific, and political advisers whether to use the atomic bomb. Then on August 6th it was dropped on Hiroshima, killing over ninety thousand Japanese and opening the age of atomic warfare. Why? According to nuclear physicist Leo Szilard, Secretary of State James Byrnes had urged that it be dropped, not because it was needed to defeat Japan, but as an implied threat to Stalin "to make Russia more manageable in Europe." Truman later said that his primary motive had been to shorten the war and save the lives of an estimated one million American soldiers who might have had to be sacrificed in a bloody invasion of the

Japanese mainland. Critics argued that no such invasion was necessary, since Japan was already seeking to surrender through Russia. According to the Office of the Chief of Military History, Department of the Army, some considered the real purpose of the hasty decision to use the bomb, three full months before any scheduled invasion of Japan, a political one—to end the war quickly before Russia could get into it, thus freezing Stalin out of a US-controlled postwar occupation of Japan.

Two days after the Hiroshima attack, Stalin declared war on Japan and launched a powerful offensive against the Japanese armies in Manchuria. The following day a second atomic bomb was dropped on Nagasaki, killing almost seventy-four thousand more Japanese. Tokyo sued for peace next day, and on August 14th Truman announced Japan's surrender. Stalin saw victory as a Russian revenge for his country's defeat in 1904 by Japan. "Forty years have we, the people of the old generation, waited for this day!" he declared in Moscow. Now the complete Russian patriot, he identified the old defeat of the Tsar's armies with the honor of the Soviet Union. Scooping up three hundred thousand Japanese prisoners, Stalin turned them over to the Red Chinese.

The news about America's new atomic bomb was played down in the Soviet press as much as possible, on Stalin's orders. He did not want a frightened Russian people weakening the bold hand he knew he would now have to play at the peace table. But he lost no time in assigning the highest priority to Soviet nuclear research, organizing a special ministry to speed the development of atomic weapons, rocketry and space research. Not only would he overtake the Americans, he vowed, but he would *surpass* them and dazzle the whole world! Three months after Japan's surrender Molotov made a blustering speech warning that the secrets of the atom were no secrets at all: "We shall have atomic energy and much else!"

But Stalin was fully aware that he had a long way to go to catch up to his chief world rival. "We know we are behind in many things," he admitted to General Eisenhower on August 12th, as they stood together on top of the Lenin Mausoleum reviewing a parade of Red youth. "And we know that you can help us." But America continued to refuse him the big postwar loan he needed. American opposition also blocked him from stripping Germany of the millions in reparations he sought. Stalin utilized the only way left to him to get the USSR back on its feet economically—control and plunder of the highly developed countries of East Europe held by the Red Army.

In Poland, Hungary, Romania, Bulgaria, and Albania, one after the other, he established puppet regimes run by Communists trained in Moscow. All were police states, sealed off from contact or communication with the West. Then Stalin began to milk these satellites for whatever Russia needed but made the mistake of trying to bully Yugoslavia into line with them. Tito promptly went to Moscow to protest, and found himself with Stalin at a drinking party in the Kremlin. "There's still strength in me!" Stalin shouted jovially. Slipping his hands under Tito's armpits, he lifted the tough Yugoslav off the floor three times in tune to a Russian folk melody.

Stalin had another purpose in extending Communist borders deep into Europe. If attack came again from the West, he was determined that this time Soviet soil would not furnish the battleground. The international political climate between East and West grew chillier. On September 11th, a meeting of a newly created Council of Foreign Ministers broke up in failure, unable to agree on a peace treaty. Truman now became worried by Stalin's increasingly belligerent attitude. Alarmed over America's rapid demobilization while Stalin kept the Red Army at wartime strength, Truman asked Congress for a peacetime draft. On February 28th, America officially acknowledged the Cold War as Byrnes announced a "get tough with Russia" policy.

Five days later, Winston Churchill, no longer Prime Minister of Britain, made a famous speech while visiting Fulton,

Missouri. "From Stettin in the Baltic to Trieste in the Adriatic," he declared, "an iron curtain has descended across the continent. . . . This is certainly not the liberated Europe we fought to build up." He added, "I do not believe that Soviet Russia desires war. What they desire is the fruits of war and the indefinite expansion of their power and doctrines. From what I have seen of our Russian friends and allies, I am convinced that there is nothing they admire so much as strength . . . nothing for which they have less respect than weakness."

Churchill's "Iron Curtain" speech created an uproar. Stalin issued a May Day order to the Red Army, warning, "We should not forget for a single minute the intrigues of international reaction, which is hatching plans for a new war." He ordered a propaganda offensive against the United States, charging America with military imperialism in Latin America and China, and calling upon workers of all countries to protest against the instigators of a new war.

On September 6th, Byrnes declared from Stuttgart that American policy was now one of helping "the German people to win their way back to an honorable place among the free and peace-loving nations of the world." One week later, US Secretary of Commerce Henry A. Wallace bitterly attacked Byrnes for this speech, and criticized US foreign policy for becoming "imperialistic," arousing Russian fear, suspicion, and distrust. Truman angrily demanded Wallace's resignation, confirming Stalin's cynicism about American intentions. "What is one to make," he asked Molotov acidly, "of a nation which now fawns on its former enemy as a respectable ally—and snarls at its former ally as a dangerous enemy?" But Stalin saw nothing reprehensible in his own power grab in East Europe.

Hoping to ease East-West misunderstandings, British Field-Marshal Bernard Montgomery visited the Kremlin on January 6, 1947, tendering some gifts to his host. "You bring me these presents," the dictator smiled wryly. "What do you want of me?"

Montgomery said he wanted Stalin to believe that there was no secret military alliance or plot between England and America. "I don't in the least object to one," Stalin shrugged, "provided it is *not* directed against the Soviet Union."

Truman asked Congress for four hundred million dollars in military and economic aid to Greece and Turkey, making it clear that America now reserved the right to intervene in the affairs of foreign nations threatened by Communism. Stalin considered the Truman Doctrine an American pretext for ringing the Soviet Union with US military bases. He was further embittered when Truman's new Secretary of State, George C. Marshall, announced a 12,000,000,000 dollar program of American foreign aid for the economic recovery of Western Europe. Stalin saw the Marshall Plan as a maneuver to strengthen West Europe against him.

His adviser in plotting countermoves was Colonel General Andrei Zhdanov, hero of Leningrad and in 1947 the most powerful voice on foreign policy in the Politburo. Zhdanov persuaded Stalin to use the Communist International to denounce the Marshall Plan as "Wall Street imperialism," inspiring strikes and mass demonstrations against it, especially in politically unstable Italy and France. What the Plan really represented, Zhdanov explained, was a desperate attempt by Truman to create an artificial market for American industry, which was now struggling against a postwar depression. The Soviet propaganda mill began to grind out millions of pamphlets describing the sordid horrors of workers' lives in US cities, where their wages were too slim to buy an overcoat ouce in six years, and where their wives found it an almost impossible task to obtain enough food to feed their families. Apparently even Stalin himself was convinced because he told one American visitor, "The Soviet Union can use many thousands of qualified mechanics, and we will guarantee any American mechanic willing to go to Russia the highest possible American standard of living."

On September 18, 1947, Vishinsky rose in the United Nations to attack US policy as leading to war, and he lashed out at America's high officials as warmongers. One Soviet publication published an article comparing Truman to Hitler, accusing him of having betrayed Roosevelt's policies "by letting a military and Wall Street coalition dictate atomic diplomacy in a new drive for world domination." Washington, in turn, became increasingly suspicious of and hostile toward Stalin. The State Department began to orient American defence policy toward an anti-Soviet military partnership with a rearmed West Germany as the core of a "European Defence Force."

Rising anti-Communist sentiment in America led Truman to order a loyalty investigation of all Federal employees. The FBI uncovered several Americans spying for Russia. The Justice Department prosecuted eleven acknowledged leaders of the American Communist Party, who were jailed. American ultraconservatives were not slow to take advantage of political opportunities afforded by the Cold War climate. Senator Joseph McCarthy of Wisconsin created an uproar with Senate hearings that sought to label as subversive a variety of American liberals, anti-Fascists, State Department "eggheads" and college professors; while in the House, a Committee on Un-American Activities (HUAC) held hearings to ferret out Communism in Hollywood. Senator McCarthy ultimately began to accuse the whole Democratic Party, the Secretary of the Army, and even Dwight D. Eisenhower, as Red dupes or Moscow agents, until he finally exasperated the US Senate into passing a vote of condemnation against him and his tactics. But until his downfall, "McCarthyism" badly frightened the nation's intellectuals in Washington, in universities and high schools, in the theatre and other professions, making them afraid to speak out on controversial issues for fear of being denounced as Communists.

Stalin was cynically amused at the anti-Communist hysteria he had inspired among Americans. His genuine subversion was at work in France and Italy, where Zdhanov had spurred the Cominform to organize paralyzing strikes. Truman struck back by embargoing all military shipments to the Soviet bloc of nations, and his Foreign Assistance Act appropriated 5,000,000,000 dollars for a first year's aid to sixteen European nations. This aid strengthened the governments of France and Italy, and the strikes failed to bring Red regimes to power.

Frustrated at his failure to defeat the Marshall Plan in West Europe, Stalin ordered a coup in Czechoslovakia. The staunchly prodemocratic Benes government was forced out, and the Czech Communist Party took over. Now Stalin tightened his control over all the Iron Curtain countries, to wield them as a single force against the Marshall Plan bloc. All the satellites pledged complete obedience to Moscow—all, that is, except Yugoslavia. Despite threats of invasion, assassination, and economic sanctions, Marshal Tito refused to take orders from the Kremlin, insisting that Yugoslavia would remain Communist but completely independent. Stalin was outraged.

He had counted on Yugoslavia's standing army of thirty tough divisions, which had driven off their Nazi invaders without Soviet help, to help him put pressure on Italy and Greece. But what worried Stalin most was that Tito's exampie might infect the other satellites with a similar spirit of defiant independence. Tito revived his old fears of Trotsky—the dreaded symbol of a Communism which was anti-Stalin.

In a black mood, he ordered Tito's expulsion from the Cominform as a deserter from the Marxist-Leninist doctrine and the chief agent and spy of Wall Street.

15

Berlin, Korea, and the End

Zdhanov died suddenly in the summer of 1948, the Soviet Cold War strategy he had inspired a dismal failure. His place was taken by Molotov, who convinced Stalin that they could gain back all the prestige they had lost since the war by a single bold move. A land blockade to isolate the western zone of Berlin from West Germany would starve two million West Berliners into the East German camp, and freeze the Allies out of the city. It was a calculated risk, but Stalin felt sure that the West would not dare alienate world opinion by trying to shoot their way into Berlin, risking another world war.

The Berlin blockade began on June 24th. Denied access to the city by road from West Germany, the Allies made Stalin's jaw drop in chagrin by flying up to 4,500 tons of supplies into the city *every day.* The Berlin airlift continued for almost an entire year, a stunning demonstration of American power and determination. Stalin must have been reminded of his own words a quarter of a century earlier, when he had told students at the University of Sverdlov, "American efficiency is that indomitable spirit that neither knows nor will be deterred by any obstacle." He finally called off the blockade after it became apparent that it was boomeranging by uniting the West against him.

Stalin knew he had blundered on April 4, 1949, when twelve nations signed the North Atlantic Pact in Washington, agreeing that "an armed attack against one or more of them in Europe or

North America shall be considered an attack against them all." To signalize this new unity, Britain, France and the United States merged their three zones of occupation into a new, independent state recognized as West Germany. Stalin bitterly attacked this move as a violation of the Potsdam agreement, and turned his own zone of occupation into the German Democratic Republic. The Voice of America—US broadcasts beamed through the Iron Curtain—sought to explain NATO to East Europeans, but Stalin angrily ordered Western broadcasts "jammed," to prevent them from being heard in the Communist world. Failing to replace American influence by Communism in West Europe, Stalin ironically found himself succeeding where he really did not want to—in China. On December 7th, Chiang Kai-shek's forces fled to Formosa. Mainland China, under Mao Tse-tung, became the world's second great Communist power.

Far more worrisome to the American people was a startling announcement from the White House. "We have evidence," Truman told them, "that within recent weeks an atomic explosion occurred in the USSR." Despite what US scientists had tried to make the American people understand, they had persisted in believing that the A-bomb would remain a US monopoly as long as its "secrets" could be kept from Stalin's spies. They realized now that atomic weapons were available to any nation with the resources and brains to seek them.

On December 21, 1949, Russian notables and world Communist leaders jammed into the Moscow Opera House to attend a giant celebration of Stalin's seventieth birthday. He sat facing his own huge portrait, surrounded by flowers and flags. His son Lieutenant-General Vassily Stalin sparked the storm of applause for the Generalissimo who had led his people into the Atomic Era.

The race for atomic supremacy went into high gear. In January, 1950, Truman ordered the US Atomic Energy Commission to develop a hydrogen bomb with "superkill" power.

Stalin promptly urged his scientists to rush ahead with a Soviet H-bomb. It took the United States two years to develop and test their ultimate horror weapon; Russia had hers six months later.

Having been checkmated in the US-Soviet confrontation in Berlin, Stalin decided to even the score in another country split in half between the two rivals—Korea. Following the end of the war, Korea had been divided into two zones for occupation purposes by the 38th Parallel, which had soon frozen into an armed border. North Korea showed increasing signs of becoming an Oriental outpost of Soviet power. Its streets were plastered with huge posters of Stalin and Lenin proclaiming: "Long live Stalin, creator of our victories! . . . The Soviet Government is the highest form of Democracy . . . Long live the friendship of the Soviet Union and Korea!" The Red Army drilled North Korean troops, supplying them with Soviet tanks and weapons. Below the 38th Parallel the American Army trained and armed the South Koreans.

Stalin was outraged when Truman appealed to the UN for supervised elections in Korea to create a single national government. He accused Truman of violating a US-Soviet agreement on Korea by going to the LIN, and demanded that both sides should pull out their occupation forces. Stalin stood to gain more than just a UN halo by this apparent willingness to let Koreans settle their own affairs. The North Korean Army was far stronger, better trained and equipped than the South Korean troops. When Stalin pressed the button and they invaded South Korea, Truman would have to weaken the American military posture in Europe by rushing forces to Asia.

The UN defeated the Soviet proposal and voted instead to send a Commission to Korea. On August 15, 1948, the Republic of Korea was proclaimed in the south, recognized by Washington. Stalin countered by a setting up a "Democratic People's Republic of Korea" in the north. Then he hurled a psychological time bomb by announcing that all Soviet troops would be withdrawn by December, regardless of whether that imperialist power America chose to stay in control of South Korea.

It was a clever move. Not only did Stalin leave a powerful North Korean Army behind him, but Communist propaganda had also discredited the Syngman Rhee government as a reactionary, rich man's dictatorship, tool of American imperialism. On June 25, 1950, on signal from Stalin, North Koreans drove south across the 38th Parallel. The UN Security Council, boycotted by Soviet delegates, voted to support South Korea in driving the invaders back. Truman ordered US air and sea forces to implement the UN decision, and sent American troops as UN forces under the generalship of Commander-in-Chief Douglas MacArthur.

The war seesawed back and forth until, on November 6th, Chinese Communist troops suddenly poured across the Yalu River into North Korea, entering the war against the UN. The news delighted Stalin as much as it stunned Washington. Now American strength would be bled heavily in the Far East, and at the same time Mao Tse-tung would be kept too busy to cause Stalin any headaches in rivalry for world Communist leadership. The bitterly fought UN "police action" in Korea lasted for two years until an armistice agreement restored the 38th Parallel.

Stalin, meanwhile, had resumed the power struggle against the United States in Germany. America pressed for a reunified Germany, but Stalin refused without a guarantee that the new Germany would first be prohibited from making any military alliance with the West. When Truman would not agree, Stalin built up an East German police force of fifty thousand men, large enough for an army. Alleging that this was a violation of the Yalta and Potsdam agreements to disarm and demilitarize Germany completely, Truman set about rearming West Germany.

On May 26, 1952, the Allies signed a peace treaty with West Germany, admitting her to NATO, and guaranteeing to fight beside her if Russia attacked. Stalin was furious, seeing in this new alliance a solid front of the world's leading capitalist powers turned against him—the very threat which his old enemy Trotsky had warned would one day engulf a Communist Russia if it failed to win security by world revolution.

Stalin made his last public appearance in October, at the Nineteenth Party Congress in Moscow. Moving more slowly now, showing definite signs of age, he made a speech to prepare the Russian people for the struggle against world capitalism he now saw as inevitable. To wipe out any vestiges of pro-American sentiment, Stalin declared that the Soviet Union *alone* deserved credit for smashing the German and Japanese fascist tyranny. Now Soviet policy must take a decisive new shift, because of "the inevitability of wars between capitalistic countries." He had no wish to admit that the danger which faced Russia was of a capitalist world whose weapons were all zeroed in on the Soviet Union. The danger to peace, Stalin told his people, came from rival capitalist powers fighting each other over rich markets and raw materials.

The Soviet Union was the champion of all small nations struggling for freedom against colonialism. Stalin called for peace tactics which might prevent a particular war. Russia must break up NATO; give economic aid to the people of underdeveloped areas; and above all, support revolutionary governments everywhere. The US-USSR coexistence policy was dead, at least as far as Joseph Stalin was concerned.

Stalin hoped to capitalize on what he considered a fatal weakness in American diplomacy—automatically rushing to the opposite side of any position taken by the Soviet Union. He felt that Washington followed an almost inflexible policy of propping up any shaky government which seemed threatened by a Soviet-inspired revolution. All he had to do to provoke the United States into the trap of allying itself with unpopular dictatorships was to support the discontent of their people. Then

Cominform agents could inflame popular hatred for the American imperialists whose arms and money kept the rich, corrupt local aristocrats in power, while the Soviet Union was portrayed as the champion of freedom and social justice. Stalin found rich irony in Washington's reluctance to remind the oppressed masses in underdeveloped countries that the American way itself had been born in a fiery revolution against unjust tyranny in 1776; Stalin's agents, on the contrary, boasted of the Soviet Revolution as the model to follow in overthrowing oppressive feudal governments of Central and South America, and Southeast Asia. "Yankee Go Home!" signs were printed in many different languages all over the world, but their common inspiration was the crafty mind of Joseph Stalin.

In January, 1953, he suddenly startled the world by announcing the arrest of a group of Soviet doctors for the alleged murder of Zdhanov and for plotting against leading Army officers. High-ranking Soviet officials trembled, wondering whether another terrible mass purge was in the making. The mystery remained unsolved because of a world-shaking development two months later. It was first announced in a series of phone calls by the head of Stalin's bodyguard. One by one, Molotov, Malenkov, Nikita Khrushchev, and Lavrenti Beria, Stalin's police chief since 1938, learned the startling news. Joseph Stalin had had a stroke.

Hurrying to his bedside, they found him paralyzed and unconscious. Thinking he was dead, Beria broke into a great outburst of joy. Stalin stirred and raised an arm, whereupon Beria threw himself in terror at his master's feet, kissing Stalin's hand.

The dictator's children were summoned to his deathbed—his daughter Svetlana, now thirty, and Air Force Lieutenant-General Vassily, thirty-two—but he never regained consciousness to bid them farewell. Bearded priests of the Russian Orthodox Church called special services to pray for the mighty leader who had lived and was dying as a confirmed atheist.

On March 5, 1953, at 9:50 p.m. Thursday night, seventy-three-year-old Joseph Vissarionovich Djugashvili, alias Koba, alias Stalin, died of a brain hemorrhage.

The great, terrible Stalin dynasty was over.

Throughout Russia huge crowds gathered around loudspeakers and bulletin boards, whispering and often sobbing over the Kremlin communique: "The heart of the comrade and inspired continuer of Lenin's will, the wise leader and teacher of the Communist Party and the Soviet people—Joseph Vissarionovich Stalin—has stopped beating." Among those who wept publicly was Nikita Khrushchev. "Like Peter, he fought barbarism with barbarism," Khrushchev said later. "But he was a great man."

Stalin's body, dressed in his simple military tunic adorned with medals and decorations, lay in state in a hall of flowers. Hundreds of thousands of Moscow's men, women and children poured past the coffin for sixty continuous hours to view their dead leader in silent awe. Then a great funeral procession wound through Red Square, with Malenkov at the head of pallbearers who included Beria, Vassily Stalin, Molotov, Bulganin, Kaganovich and Khrushchev. As the glass-covered coffin was carried into the huge Lenin Mausoleum to lie beside Lenin's embalmed body, artillery thundered, church bells rang and factory whistles blew in final salute to the dead Communist leader.

In New York City the UN flag was lowered to half-mast. Delegates bowed their heads in one minute's silence, after delegate Andrei Vishinsky described the death of the immortal Stalin as "the most grievous loss for all human beings." In India, Prime Minister Nehru called Stalin "a man with a giant's stature and indomitable courage," judging him an influence "in favor of peace." Red China dictator Mao Tse-tung ordered three days of national mourning for "the most esteemed and dearest friend and teacher of the Chinese people."

Reaction in the West was considerably less adulatory. President Dwight D. Eisenhower said, tersely, "The thoughts of

America go out to all the people of the USSR—the men and women, the boys and girls—in the villages, cities, farms and factories of their homeland." Washington's official message to the Kremlin consisted of chilly "official condolences." *The New York Times* editorialized acidly, "Our children's children will still be paying the price for the evil which he brought into this world." The kindest American word was spoken by Loy Henderson, US Ambassador to Iran, who told the sorrowing Soviet legation there, "In one of the darkest periods of history, Joseph Stalin was a staunch ally to the United States."

In London, Winston Churchill was stubbornly, eloquently silent, while the Labor Party's Herbert Morrison described Stalin as "a great man but not a good man." In Rome, the Vatican asked Roman Catholics to pray for the soul of the late Red dictator who had persecuted them mercilessly, but who now "must account to the Almighty for his actions."

So died the shoemaker's son who had torn away a fourth of the earth from the capitalist camp and made it Communist—an empire larger by far than any dreamed of by all the Tsars of Russia. No tyrant of history ever sought or amassed so vast a power. He belonged to the breed of great revolutionary despots like Cromwell, Robespierre, and Napoleon, beginning as the servant of revolution and making himself its master. Posing as the great champion of the oppressed Russian masses, he killed millions of them without a twinge of remorse, and enslaved millions more in the name of Communist liberty.

Yet he also transformed feudal peasants and workers from Asiatic barbarians into trained citizens of Europe's leading modern industrial power, second in the world only to the United States, in an amazing twenty-nine brief years. He brainwashed the Russian people politically, and isolated them from the full truth about the West behind an Iron Curtain. Yet he also changed them from illiterate, uncultured masses into an educated population eagerly interested in art, ballet, and music, with so great a love and respect for classic literature that today no nation on earth reads more copies of Shakespeare, Byron, Dickens, Balzac, Goethe, Hugo, and Zola.

Paradoxically, it was Stalin, product of a medieval feudal society, who created a Russian scientific community so advanced that it was able to become the first nation in the world to orbit men in space. And the Russian people could never forget that it was Stalin who had inspired and led them to victory against the mightiest army of invaders in history.

But Stalin's successors lost no time in attacking and destroying many of the hated, tyrannical aspects of his reign, while continuing to build on the giant economic structure he had erected for the Russian people. Stalin's chief executioner, Beria, was arrested and shot less than four months after Stalin's death. When Nikita Khrushchev eventually emerged as the new Kremlin boss, he startled both the West and the Communist world by making "de-Stalinization" official Soviet policy.

Denouncing Stalin as a tyrant and murderer, and accusing him of self-glorification through a "cult of personality," Khrushchev ordered Stalin's name expunged from Soviet history books, cities and street signs. In 1961 he even removed Stalin's body from its proud resting place in the red and black Lenin Mausoleum to an ignominious grave behind it under the Kremlin walls. Yet when this thaw in Stalinism encouraged the people of Hungary and other satellites to revolt against their own Stalin-appointed Red tyrants, Khrushchev crushed them ruthlessly with Soviet forces, blustering angrily, "As against imperialists, we are all Stalinists!" He did, however, reverse Stalin's policy of preparing for a new world holocaust as inevitable, and pledged the USSR to seek a new coexistence policy with the United States instead.

An outraged Red China split with Russia on this issue, dividing the Communist world into two rival camps. This was the very Kremlin nightmare Stalin had schemed to prevent by sabotaging Mao Tse-tung's rise to power for as long as he had been able, and which now, paradoxically, had been brought about by Red China's loyalty to him after death. One month after Khrushchev himself had been deposed by Leonid Brezhnev and Aleksei Kosygin, Mao Tse-tung indicated his hopes for a Soviet return to the anti-Western policy of Stalin's last years by sending a Red delegation to Moscow in November, 1964. With great deliberation, Red Chinese Premier Chou En-lai marched behind the Lenin Mausoleum to lay a defiant wreath on Stalin's downgraded final resting place. Soon afterward, Russian historians were ordered to stop picturing Stalin as Khrushchev's archvillain, and to report his role in Soviet history more objectively.

On December 20, 1964, a windswept Sunday commemorating the eighty-fifth anniversary of Stalin's birthday, his grave was again visited, and the simple headstone decorated with three bouquets of red, white and yellow flowers, placed there by three of Russia's 226,253,000 people who remembered him with affection.

Bibliography

Barbusse, Henri. *Stalin.* New York: The Macmillan Company, 1935.

Barghoorn, Frederick C. *The Soviet Image of the United States.* New York: Harcourt, Brace and Company, 1950.

Basseches, Nikolaus. *Stalin.* London and New York: Staples Press, 1952.

Carr, Albert Z. *Truman, Stalin and Peace.* Garden City, New York: Doubleday & Company, Inc., 1950.

Constitution (Fundamental Law) of the Union of Soviet Socialist Republics. Moscow: Foreign Languages Publishing House, 1962.

Conte, Arthur. *Yalta ou Le Partage du Monde.* Paris: Laffont, 1963.

Davies, Joseph E. *Mission to Moscow.* New York: Simon and Schuster, 1941.

Deutscher, Isaac. *Stalin: A Political Biography.* New York:Vintage Books, 1962. Douglas, William O. *Russian Journey.* Garden City, NewYork: Doubleday & Company, Inc., 1956. Dulles, Allen. *The Craft of Intelligence.* New York: Harper& Row, Publishers, Inc., 1963. Duranty, Walter. *I Write As I Please.* New York: Halcyon House, 1935.

Fischer, Louis. *The Life of Lenin.* New York, Evanston, and London: Harper & Row, Publishers, Inc., 1964.

Greenfield, Kent Roberts, editor. *Command Decisions.* (Department of the Army.) New York: Harcourt, Brace and Company, 1959.

Halacy, D. S., Jr. *1936.* Derby, Connecticut: Monarch Books, 1963.

Heilbroner, Robert L. *The Worldly Philosophers.* New York: Simon and Schuster, 1953.

Hicks, Granville. *One of Us: John Reed.* New York: Equinox Cooperative Press, Inc., 1935.

Hindus, Maurice. *Crisis in the Kremlin*. Garden City, New York: Doubleday & Company, Inc., 1953.

Kennan, George F. *Russia and the West*. Boston and Toronto: Little, Brown and Company, 1961.

Lauterbach, Richard E. *These Are the Russians*. New York: Harper & Brothers Publishers, 1945.

Montgomery, Bernard Law. *The Memoirs of Field-Marshal Montgomery*. Cleveland: The World Publishing Company, 1958.

Moorehead, Alan. *The Russian Revolution*. New York: Harper & Brothers Publishers, 1958.

Neal, Fred Warner. *US Foreign Policy and the Soviet Union*. Santa Barbara, California: Center for the Study of Democratic Institutions, 1961.

Seldes, George. *The Great Quotations*. New York: Lyle Stuart, Inc., 1960.

Shirer, William L. *The Rise and Fall of the Third Reich*.

New York: Simon and Schuster, 1962. Souvarine, Boris. *Stalin*. New York: Longmans, Green & Co., 1939.

Spolansky, Jacob. *The Communist Trail in America*. New York: The Macmillan Company, 1951. Taylor, A. J. P. *The Origins of the Second World War*. New York: Atheneum Publishers, 1961. Thayer, Charles W. *Russia*. New York. Time Inc., 1963.

Trotsky, Leon. *Stalin*. New York and London: Harper & Brothers Publishers, 1941.

Trotsky, Leon. *The Russian Revolution*. Garden City, New York: Doubleday & Company, Inc., 1959.

Truman, Harry S. *1945: Year of Decisions*. Garden City, New York: Doubleday & Company, Inc., 1955.

Truman, Harry S. *1946–1952: Years of Trial and Hope*. Garden City, New York: Doubleday & Company, Inc., 1956.

Werth, Alexander. *Russia at War*. New York: E. P. Dutton & Company, 1964.

"Killer of the Masses." *Time*, March 16, 1953.

"Sick Joke." *Time,* April 17, 1964.

"The Battle over the Tomb." *Time,* April 24, 1964.

"That Russian Gold." *Time,* May 15, 1964.

Index